PRISON POETRY

Scott T.K Keighran

Prison Poetry

Copyright © Scott T.K Keighran 2023

The Author has asserted their rights under the Copyright Act 1968 (the Act) to be identified as the author of this work.

All rights reserved. No part of this publication may be reproduced, stored in a retrieval system, or transmitted in any form or by any means, electronic, mechanical, photocopying, recording or otherwise, without the prior written permission of the author. Any person who does any unauthorised act in relation to this publication may be liable to criminal prosecution and civil claims for damages.

The Australian Copyright Act 1968 (the Act) allows a maximum of one chapter or ten per cent of this book, whichever is the greater, to be photocopied for educational purposes by an educational institution holding a statutory education licence provided that the educational institution (or body that administers it) has given a remuneration notice to the Copyright Agency (Australia) under the Act.

ISBN: 978-1-922784-75-9 (Paperback)

A catalogue record for this book is available from the National Library of Australia

Self-Published by Scott T.K Keighran, with assistance by Clark & Mackay

Proudly printed in Australian by Clark & Mackay

Contents

Preface v

Coming In 1
Persistence 9
Jail Fit 17
The Time Is Now 27
Recidivism 37
When Your Number's Up 47
An Ode to Harley 53
The Sentence Falls 63
Prison Politics 71

Self-Destruction 79

Recurring Dreams 87

Coming Back 95

Adversity 105

Missing Home 119

Karma 127

Day In, Day Out 135

Your Poem 147

Party Animal 153

Christmas Day 161

Doubt 169

Riot! Riot! Riot! 177

Ambivalence 183

This Is Me 191

Dark Days 197

Diamond Life 205

Going Home 215

Preface

I have written this book gradually over several years while incarcerated in the NSW prison system. I had no intention of writing a book when I wrote the first poem. I had no intention to ever write a poem until the moment I started writing it. It just happened – an organic process that was both unexpected and a long time coming. I would describe the poetry as a journal of sorts that details my thoughts, experiences, and philosophies. The book gives an insight into what life's like in prison, the pitfalls of a life of crime, how it feels to go through the whole experience, the thought process I've gone through, and the lessons learnt along the way.

I've spent over seven years incarcerated in total for various serious offences. I grew up in the western suburbs of Sydney, and I was attracted to the life of crime, spending time associated with an outlaw motorcycle gang (OMCG).

I have suffered and caused a lot of pain and adversity as a result of the choices I've made. I've hurt a lot of people, carving my path of self-destruction, and faced some hard truths along the way. I give an honest account of my experiences. This is my story told in a unique way.

I don't have any tertiary qualifications. The opinions I share are purely based on my experiences and what I know to be true for myself. I hope that the content can be of some benefit to whoever reads it, along with being an interesting read, offering an eye-opening view into another world. Enjoy.

Coming In

Coming into prison for the first time is a daunting experience, no matter who you are. We all have our own conceptions about what goes on in prison. Once it becomes a reality that you are actually coming in, your mind naturally starts imagining those worst case scenarios. Anxiety takes hold of you, and it all becomes very real, very quickly.

The process once you've been arrested and taken to the police station is as follows.

If the police deny bail, you'll go before a judge either that day or the following one, depending on the time of your arrest and how busy the court is. If you were arrested at 7 pm, for instance, after court hours, it will obviously be the following day. That's unless it's a weekend, or worse still, Friday night. Then you'll usually have to wait until Monday morning, and you'll be held in the police cells until then. When you front the magistrate, they'll either grant bail and you'll go home until you're due to appear for your next scheduled court date; or if bail is refused, you will be held in custody to front court on that scheduled date.

Once you've been refused bail, you'll be handed over to corrective services custody and held in holding cells, where you'll wait for days – or even weeks – to be transported to prison. Most of you would've seen the prison transport trucks driving around with the tiny little windows and blue and white reflective trim around the sides. Those trucks aren't all that big, but they hold up to 20 people at a time. They are dirty and very claustrophobic. One of these transport trucks will pick you up and cart you off to a prison. Upon arrival, each new inmate is stripped completely naked and searched for contraband. All personal clothing is confiscated and prison greens are issued. Before being sent to the general prison population, each new inmate must be assessed by a doctor, a welfare officer, and corrective services officers to determine where an inmate should be housed.

This process usually takes a few days but can drag out to several weeks if the inmate is coming down off drugs, is suicidal, or has mental health or other health issues. The units where new inmates are housed while going through this process are horrible. They are very loud, with people yelling and screaming coming down off drugs, having psychotic episodes, or just pissed off. The cells are filthy, with nothing in them but a bunk bed, toilet, and shower. You have to share the cell with someone who may be coming down off drugs, stinks, is angry, upset, depressed, suicidal, scared, etc. Everyone is locked in cell for most, if not all of the day with no TV, radio, magazines, newspaper, pen, paper... No nothing! Four walls and a stinky cellmate for days and weeks on end.

Once that process is over and all the assessments are complete, we are taken to the general population units, pods, or 'main,' as they are also known. From the moment of your arrest up until walking into the main, your mind does not stop racing, wondering what may happen when you walk into that yard. That whole time is spent mentally preparing for what may await. Once that time does come when you walk into the unit or yard, everyone susses the newcomers out. It's an intimidating experience to have up to a hundred prisoners size you up at once.

I was 29 when I first came to prison. I was 105 kg, fit, and strong, having trained weights my whole adult life, and I can look after myself fairly well. Yet, it was daunting. I was worried just the same as anyone else who is going through that experience for the first time. I know some very tough and capable men who have no dramas whatsoever looking after themselves who say the same thing of their first day walking into the main.

I made sure I held my head up to show I wasn't scared or intimidated. I didn't want to come across as weak or an easy target. Nothing happened. It rarely ever does but the guy walking in for the first time doesn't know that. Usually, the only time someone new coming in has an issue is if they either come in with the wrong attitude or bump into someone who they have an issue with from outside. Maybe a rival gang, crew, or family. Sometimes, an unfortunate new arrival gets targeted for some reason. It does happen but not often.

Those first few days are all about finding your feet and just wrapping your head around the situation, learning how things work (prison politics which is another chapter later in the book), and settling in. It doesn't take long before the initial anxiety subsides, but there is always an underlying tension in prison. This is especially so while on remand. Remand is when you're in custody, bail refused, but you are not convicted of the offence you've been charged with. Inmates on remand are still waiting for their case to be heard at trial or sentencing. On remand, everyone is stressed, having recently come into custody with new charges. No one knows how long they will be inside, whether or not they will get bail at their next attempt, be convicted at trial, or beat the charges. The uncertainty is very stressful. Guys are adjusting to being separated from kids, partners, and families. Everyone is stressing about money, finding a good lawyer, being fired, losing the house, or being divorced. For some, it's the shame of being labelled a criminal on the news and in the newspaper, along with all sorts of other shit going on in their lives that have just being turned upside down. Then there are others dealing with drug and alcohol dependency, adjusting to being without their poison, trying to fill that void with whatever they can get their hands on. Some have mental health issues, and others just don't cope. With all this going on and up to a hundred people living on top of one another dealing with the same shit, the place is a pressure cooker. It can be chaotic and very stressful conditions.

    I think most would agree that coming into custody, being on remand, the uncertainty of not knowing what's going to happen or how long you'll be stuck in limbo with your life on hold is the worst part of the sentence.

    On remand, you'll usually be housed as a maximum security inmate, unless the charges are very minor. As a maximum security inmate, we spend around 18–19 hours of each day locked in cell. With all this time laying around in cell, you can't help but do head miles. Doing head miles refers to stressing, continually thinking about what's happened, and wishing you could change things, as well as worrying about what's going to happen in the future. You get stuck in this loop going over everything in your mind again and again. Trust me when I say, you'll do a lot of head miles those first few months. Eventually, though, you wrap your head around your situation and accept that this is how things are for a while.

Coming into prison for the first time is a major shock to the system. There is a lot going on, and it's likely the worst thing you've ever dealt with, in the worst place you've ever been, suffering the worst stress you've ever experienced, while at least initially being as afraid as you've ever been. That's what coming to prison for the first time feels like.

Welcome to the jungle.

> *'I am an old man and I have known a great many troubles, but most of them never happened.'*
>
> —Mark Twain

Coming In

I don't know what to expect.
Everything has gone all wrong.
I never thought I'd end up in prison.
I've made mistakes, but here I don't belong.

Sitting in the holding cells,
I start the mental preparation.
For the transport truck to arrive,
That will deliver me to an unwelcome destination.

Anxiety takes hold of me.
What will I be walking into?
Wondering what horrors await,
I can't even begin to.

Walking through the intake gate,
I'm nervous; my mind begins to race.
What will these next moments bring?
Will I have to fight to find my place?

It's already bad enough.
I'm dealing with my legal problems.
Now I've landed in the pod.
One hundred faces starring as menacing as goblins.

To show no weakness,
I hold my head up high.
I will give them nothing to exploit
By looking each one in the eye.

I find my feet quickly,
But there's no chance I can relax.
There is always tension in the air,
Without warning into chaos things can collapse.

This feels like treading water,
Working constantly to stay afloat.
How long can I keep this up,
Holding out hope for bail, a metaphorical rescue boat.

The things I took for granted,
I now appreciate and miss so dearly.
If only I could turn back time,
I now see things so clearly.

But this is no fairytale.
I'm stuck in this situation.
I've got some road ahead to travel,
Not some place but time's the destination.

Persistence

Failing at anything sucks. Losing sucks. Obvious statements, I know. Nobody enjoys losing a big game. No one's ever happy about a business failing, a relationship breaking down, making a bad investment, or getting dropped from a team. It's painful to set big goals, having high hopes for success only to fall short, especially after putting in the time, hard work, and energy it took to get there.

This doesn't only apply to goals. Any situation where you feel as though things aren't working out the way you'd like can make you feel like a failure. The greatest sense of failure I've ever felt was coming back to prison for the current sentence I'm now serving. In the past, I've lost a football grand final, and I've been defeated in a big martial arts tournament back when I used to compete, experiencing the sharp sting of failure. However, nothing has come even remotely close to how I felt returning to prison this time around. I again let down my son, family, friends, as well as myself.

When we fail, especially after multiple times, it attacks our confidence, our self-worth. It's demotivating as well as very disappointing. It can be difficult to hold on to the desire to keep going with whatever it is your trying to achieve. That negative voice can get loud, the self-talk becoming defeatist. The thing to remember is that everyone fails. Everyone experiences the same feelings of self-doubt. No one is immune to it. The difference between those who overcome defeat or setbacks and go on to succeed over those who don't is that the success stories muster the mental strength to overcome the disappointment of failure and persist in spite of it.

Michael Jordan didn't make the high school basketball team in his sophomore year. The fucking greatest basketball player and most iconic athlete of all time didn't make the team. Can you imagine if he let his disappointment get the better of him? The world would never have known the great Air Jordan. That year, rather than playing for the varsity team, he was placed in the lower junior varsity division. He was devastated at being left off the roster and went home crying that night. But despite the crushing disappointment he felt, Michael worked hard that year, determined to prove himself. He believed that he belonged on that team. He persisted following his dream making the team the following year, and the rest is history.

Persistence is the greatest attribute a person can possess in my opinion. Perseverance, persistence, never say die, the relentless pursuit of a dream. This quality in a person will rocket them to succeed in whatever endeavour they undertake. There will always be obstacles and failures along the way. There will always be more naturally talented competition than you, but it's the one willing to work the hardest the longest who will make it in the end. The most disciplined. The one who is willing to suffer the setbacks and keep showing up. Persistence and sustained effort is what it takes. Hard work beats talent in the long run.

Persistence and change

Making big changes in your life for the better is never easy and will usually require a certain amount of persistence. Regardless of how difficult it may be or how long it takes, it is possible with desire and effort. Overcoming an addiction, for example, or a bad habit such as with alcohol or drugs, smoking, or gambling, is often a very difficult change to make. Despite knowing that change is for the best and the issue is causing problems in your life, the rational thought process is drowned out by the enormity of the task of overcoming the problem. We become comfortable with what's familiar, even if what's familiar is terrible, making us unhappy, or doing us harm.

Another example of this might be staying in an abusive relationship, because although the conditions at home are horrible, the uncertainty of leaving is terrifying. Domestic violence abuse is a complex and serious issue. I use it here to highlight the point that even in a situation as tough as many women unfortunately find themselves in, the fear of making the change to remove themselves from the abuse can be just as frightening as the abuse itself.

For many, change can be so scary after living a certain way for so long, regardless of the situation from which the change is required. The fear of change itself can be no different than any other phobia. Someone with a long-term addiction can find the thought of living a sober existence terrifying, despite hating their current life situation. I've spent years living with people in prison who have every kind of problem you can possibly imagine. Every addiction for every poison out there. Some who have kicked their habits long ago, others just getting started, and plenty in between each end of that spectrum. One thing that almost everyone says is that quitting is hard. Very hard. It is often a long-running battle with many failed attempts along the way. The ones who succeed just kept trying time and time again. After each failure, they gave it another go, until they'd finally done it.

In 2017, I was in custody on remand for another offence and was using multiple drugs to get through a really tough time (I go into it in a later chapter, so won't double up on that), but I gave it up cold turkey without any issue. I was very determined, and despite having been as sick as a dog for weeks, I persisted, stuck it out, and kicked both drug habits together. However, about a year later, I used Xanax again, which was one of the drugs I had quit. It was a contributing factor to me committing the current offence for which I'm now serving this sentence. Although I haven't used the drug for a long time now, nor do I have any intention or desire to, I have to keep working hard every day on the healthy path I'm on, focused on my goals so that if that temptation ever does arise, I can navigate the urge. It just takes effort and persistence.

Making big changes often requires sustained effort over a long period of time. The same is true of any success you strive for. Persisting despite failing many times is key along the road to seeing it done. Whatever it may be, with relentless effort and persistence, there is nothing that cannot be overcome. Persistence and effort is what it takes, along with the belief that you can succeed.

'There may be no heroic connotation to the word persistence, but the quality is to the character of man what carbon is to steel.'

—Napoleon Hill

'Energy and persistence conquer all things.'

—Benjamin Franklin

Persistence

No one likes to fail.
It's easy to feel like we should quit.
To strive for something,
And not succeed makes us feel so shit.

Why bother trying
To follow my dreams, only to end with pain.
It's taken so long to get nowhere.
Is it even worth trying again?

I'll let you in on a secret,
Something every successful person knows to be true.
Failures not always a bad thing,
But a tool to make work for you.

Winning is built off failure,
A part of the process to achieving your dreams.
Persisting through the disappointment
Lays a foundation for success as strong as structural beams.

So when facing hardship
And obstacles make goals seem so far away,
One foot in front of the other,
Keep going for tomorrow is another day.

It takes great strength
To continue toiling when facing great resistance,
But something all winners know
Is there's no better quality in man than persistence.

Jail Fit

With all this spare time on our hands in here, what to do with it? For most, drugs make the time tick by a lot quicker, killing the boredom. Drug use is rife in prison, but not everyone in prison wants to use drugs. However, a lot of people leave gaol with a drug habit who didn't have one when they first came in. People play cards, work shitty jobs in the prison, and make calls home to kids, wives, and friends. None of which is all that constructive. Some read; not a lot though. I discovered a love of reading in prison which has been transformative. The only thing that I've gotten as much out of as I've gained through reading is fitness training. I can't speak highly enough about the benefits of a good exercise routine, not just here in prison but for anyone anywhere. For many in prison, this is how we make the best use of our time. Fitness training is a big part of the prison culture and is something positive in an otherwise shitty environment, giving us something constructive to focus on.

For those at home, something as simple as committing to getting up each morning and going for a 20-minute walk can have such a positive impact. Both physically and mentally. Getting up when you'd rather stay warm in bed, putting on your shoes, and walking out the door is a positive start to your day. Not only are you exercising your body, you've exercised your will power and accomplished something positive within five minutes of getting up. If you're capable of something more strenuous, then do that. The further out of your comfort zone you're willing to push yourself, the greater the benefit.

In prison, as well as killing boredom, training is a good distraction from the stress and troubles we are experiencing. There is a mountain of medical evidence supporting the mental health benefits of regular physical exercise. Nowhere is that stress relief needed more than in prison. This environment can be toxic and incredibly stressful, and a lot of people just can't cope with it. This is a major contributing factor to the massive drug problem and the high suicide rates within the system. It is a fucking stressful environment. Another motivation is obviously to get in good shape. We all want to get out with a six pack and build some solid muscle. Plus, it pays to be fit and strong, should we get in a fight.

I've been involved in sports from the age of five. As a teenager, I began lifting weights to add some bulk for football, as I was a skinny kid, and have continued that weight training into my adult life. It felt natural to get involved with the guys who were training when I came into prison, and it was a good way to meet a few like-minded people. It also helps to be friends with other strong, fit guys who will have your back should you need it and for them to have another solid guy on their side in return.

In most maximum security prisons, the access to weights is either very limited or not allowed at all. Most of the exercise is body weight based, something similar to a CrossFit circuit. Most yards have a chin-up and dip bar but not a lot more, so this CrossFit style is the type of training I got into. Anyone who's ever tried CrossFit or F-45 style training will know it is fucking hard. It's also very satisfying. That feeling of satisfaction comes from pushing yourself through something hard, keeping on going when it hurts and you want to quit. But rather than quitting, you muster the strength to continue in spite of the pain. Together, you are exercising and developing your body as well as your will power, and it feels great. It's incredibly good for you.

Very quickly, I became fitter and stronger. I was enjoying pushing myself further and for longer periods of time. When I first started, I would stop when I was in pain and tired, hands on hips, sucking in the deep ones, wishing for the session to end. Slowly, I began to push myself beyond that point. Only a little at first, then further and further. The pain and suffering weren't getting any less – in fact, it got worse the harder I pushed – but I was able to withstand it and push on. Not only was my body growing in strength, but my mind as well. My mental toughness and resilience were improving with each workout. The will to continue became greater than the desire to quit. The positive mindset of never say die and my will to keep pushing eventually won out over the negative voice until it just shut up. I learnt to overcome the negative voice that pops up when something gets hard, telling us to quit. I also learnt that when I thought I was spent with nothing more to give, I actually had plenty more in the tank, despite what my negative mind was saying. Once I tapped into this, it wasn't long before I was doing double and triple the workload. This was something I thought impossible only months before.

This is when I started to contemplate the power of the mind, our will power, and what's possible when we really apply ourselves, not only with physical exertion, but with any endeavour we undertake. The crucible of hard physical training is just the perfect vehicle for developing these attributes that can be called upon in any area of our lives at any time. That negative voice that pops up during the workouts is the exact same one that we hear during anything else difficult we endure. It is one and the same. Therefore, the remedy is the same as well. Once you learn how to deal with it and overcome the negativity, that will almost certainly rear its ugly head during any other kind of adversity you suffer. It's not such an overwhelming task to conquer it and press on. With each workout that you encounter this fucking pest of a voice, you'll get a little better at shutting it down. Our willpower is no different to the muscles that are growing in strength with each training session. The more the will is tested under load, the stronger it gets. Adversity is life's weight set. When exposed to heavy loads, we grow stronger as we shoulder the burden. This builds character and resilience, which we can draw upon the next time we experience hardship. If we can simply adjust the way we view these hardships in our lives as something that we can learn and grow from, rather than something that has unfairly and unjustly happened to us, then just like the pain and hurt that allows our bodies to grow fitter and stronger from working out, as can the mind from life's adversities.

I really believe with every ounce of my being in the benefits of exercising on mental health, specifically in building this mental toughness that can be drawn upon when needed during tough times. it builds confidence and belief in yourself. It forms strong habits and instils an ethos of not quitting and seeing things through. Resilience, perseverance, mental strength, and a positive mindset. What better way to achieve these life changing attributes that are impossible not to benefit from, all while getting in great shape.

Another important aspect to this growth and self-development is positive self-talk, which is the remedy I touched on prior to the negative voice. If you let that negative voice get too loud, it will defeat you. I enjoy running. I suck at it, but that's why I love it. I really have to push myself to keep going. I want to stop 20 or so minutes into it. I hear that voice pop up saying 'fuck this' fairly early on. I set a distance, and whatever time I get, I'll try to improve upon it each subsequent run. It's not fun, I don't enjoy it at the time, but I do enjoy the feeling of pushing through that period when I want to stop. Once the run is over and I've improved upon the previous time, I feel great, especially when I think back to the portions of the run when I was dealing with the negative voice telling me that I couldn't be fucked doing this. It's extremely satisfying. Without fail, on each run, there is a point where I have to deal with the voice and counter it. When it says, 'Fuck this,' I say 'Fuck quitting. I will die before I quit.' When it says, 'Why am I doing this?' I counter with, 'Because I can. Because I want to succeed. If I can push through this, I can push through anything, no fucking problem.' It may sound stupid, but it works. It's very empowering, it gives me access to deeper stores of energy, and most importantly, it's forming the habit of talking down that negativity rather than having it talk me down. For any negativity my weak mind throws up, I counter it with positivity immediately. I don't allow it to get a foothold or occupy any space in my head. The positive mind is exponentially more powerful than the negative mind. The positive self-talk will drown out the negative if you believe it. The way you develop that belief is through practice and experience.

Work out every day, push yourself, and you'll have all the practice and experience you'll need when life throws you a curveball. Belief and confidence grow from experience. Give it a go. Start small and build on it each day. If that means starting with that 20-minute walk, then start there. Each day, try to go a little further in that 20 minutes, or add an extra couple of minutes. Develop the mindset to go a little further, try a little harder, push a bit more each and every day. The small, incremental daily gains add up to big leaps over the weeks and months. Build up to running a few minutes, then half of it, then all of it. If you can't run, then swim, row, or cycle. Learn to push yourself a little out of your comfort zone. When that negative voice pops up, have your counter comments ready to shut it down. Learn to draw energy from defeating that voice. It's so powerful. It doesn't take long, regardless of your start point, to build up to a decent volume, so long as you add a little bit each day and stick to it. This positive self-talk is a skill that – like any other skill – requires effort and practice to develop, but it's not hard. Just start doing it. Eventually, it becomes a habit that will just occur naturally. It crushes the negative voice as a reflex reaction and can be applied to any life situation.

The exercise, along with the positive self-talk and determination it takes to push yourself through, is not only conditioning the body but your mind as well. With your new mental toughness and resilience, you will be better equipped to deal with life's hardships. You'll tackle adversity with a wealth of experience and an arsenal of firepower. You can draw on this experience saying to yourself, 'I've got this shit.' You'll know you can endure the hard stuff, because you endure pain and suffering every single day. No fucking problem.

So, what are you capable of?

Go find out.

> *'The key to immortality is first living a life worth remembering.'*
>
> —Bruce lee

Jail Fit

Something to kill the boredom,
The routine helps to get through the day.
Physical training, pushing hard,
A chance to better myself in some way.

We exercise together.
It helps us build a bond.
It keeps us busy.
Our minds off problems and wanting to abscond.

We want to look good when we go home,
but for me, there is a deeper meaning
to push my inner limits
enduring the rigors of hard physical training.

Hitting pads, lifting weights,
CrossFit circuits, or running distance.
Not only does this build up strength,
more importantly, mental toughness and resilience.

When the voice in my head says, 'No more,'
I seize the opportunity for perseverance.
When negativity creeps into mind,
I can hurdle trouble leaving plenty of clearance.

The more arduous the workout, the better.
The pain a true gift to savour.
To muster up the strength,
To crush weakness, pushing past the point of failure.

For this is where the will power grows.
Enduring pain, I will not quit.
When life gets hard, I can draw on this.
Saying to myself, I know I've got this shit.

Never quitting becomes a habit.
The training is a metaphor for life.
Not buckling under heavy loads,
When the world decides to turn the knife

The Time Is Now

We human beings seem to be generally quite unhappy, dissatisfied creatures, despite living in an era of humanity when things have never been better. Australia is one of the highest income earning countries on earth. The cities of Sydney and Melbourne feature regularly on the world's most liveable cities' listings. We have more disposable income than any previous generation. We are not exposed to war or famine. We enjoy living under a democratic political system, benefitting from all the rights that come with it. We receive free healthcare and public education. We have a functioning welfare system, heavily subsidized medication under the PBS, free legal representation should we need it, and so much more.

Yet, despite this high standard of living, mental health issues have never been more prevalent than they are today. As a society, we have never been more depressed, stressed out, burnt out, unhappy, sick, tired, anxious, and generally dissatisfied as we are now.

Why are we so unhappy?

The poem's message is to find happiness and satisfaction in what you have now, recognising the good things in your life today rather than what you don't have and want in the future and/or dwelling on the past. I have found myself more often than I care to admit wishing I could change the past, dwelling on things that I cannot change. What a waste of mental energy and a source of mental anguish it is to spend your time thinking in this way. It can be very depressing, destructive, exhausting, and a total waste of time.

Just as often, I have been guilty of dreaming of a better tomorrow, thinking I will be happier and life will be better at some later point in time. Obviously, due to my current situation being in prison, it can be easy to get caught up thinking this way. Yet, even from my position now, it isn't helpful.

It's common for most of us to get stuck thinking this way from time to time. The reason as a society I believe we are so unhappy and dissatisfied is that our measure of success and expectations around it are exceedingly high. Even someone who considers themselves to have modest expectations and easily pleased, when asked 'What does success look like to you?' would come up with things like owning their own home, owning a business, having investment properties, an investment portfolio generating residual income. Some say being comfortable, never having to worry about money. Others want to be wealthy. All sound reasonable, maybe with the exception of the last option. The thing here is that most people especially now will struggle to own their own home. A large majority of the population are employees, not employers. Most will never own multiple investment properties, if any, nor will they build an investment portfolio capable of providing enough dividends to live off. Everyone does worry about money, and 1% of people are considered wealthy. By their own measure, they are not successful. Those who do meet these criteria are usually the most stressed and burnt out demographic. To add to this, we are constantly bombarded with all sorts of images of success that either consciously or subconsciously reinforce our lack of it. Whether we realise it or not, the message sinks in that you are not measuring up. Everyone on our social media feeds are in amazing shape, wearing designer clothes, driving a Mercedes, wearing expensive jewellery, eating at the best restaurants, partying at the best events, having the time of their lives, jet setting around the globe being the best versions of themselves. To add further insult to injury, marketing companies are making billions of dollars each and every year convincing you your life sucks and the way to make it not suck is to buy product x. They are good at it too. The companies shelling out all this money expect bang for their buck, and they get it back in spades.

Unhappy, dissatisfied consumers spend on meaningless shit in an effort to fill this void. Next year, with those profits, more billions are reinvested again on marketing, and the cycle continues.

Then you look around your social group to see your friends all getting married, buying houses, growing their families, climbing the corporate ladder, all seemingly killing it, their lives all falling into place. In reality, in most circumstances, they are buckling under crippling debt, stressed and burnt out, all while putting on a brave face trying to portray their own image of success.

Naturally, we compare ourselves and our situation against all this and feel as though we are failing. Of course, none of us want to feel like failures, and this is the cause of a great deal of the depression, anxiety, dissatisfaction, stress, and unhappiness we as a society are experiencing.

From here, it is easy to see how people get stuck thinking that things will be better in the future when certain circumstances change, whether that's earning more money, meeting the right person, getting married, buying your own home, changing jobs, working for yourself, or a thousand other reasons people think life will be better and therefore happier. So what's the remedy?

One simple method is to think about the good things in your life now. Look at what gives you happiness and satisfaction that you currently have in your life today, and be grateful for it. Our friends and family. Living in the developed world in the 21st century. The opportunities available to us. A good cup of tea. Whatever makes you happy. There is a lot to be grateful for when you just take a moment to think about it. In addition, take a moment to consider all those who aren't so lucky to enjoy all the great things that you are lucky enough to Have.

Have compassion for those people and feel a little better. Just being a human being and not an Angus beef cow bred for slaughter.

Being mindful and present and enjoying the simple things that are good in your life right now is something that anyone can benefit from today. Living in the moment or 'now' is sometimes misinterpreted as throwing caution to wind, being irresponsible, not worrying about consequences, or showing no regard for the future. This is not the case at all. Planning for the future, setting goals, and following dreams are all an important part of being happy and successful in modern life. 'The time is now' is all about making those plans, setting goals, and starting work on them. The only time you can ever act towards making them a reality is in the present moment. You can't act in the past; it's gone. The future is not guaranteed; it hasn't happened yet. The only place you'll ever be is in each present moment. The present is the only time and place where taking action is possible. Just start. By starting something you've been meaning to do, wanting to do, dreaming of doing, just by taking that step, you're already miles ahead of most. More often than not, people never take action. They spend their life dreaming and hoping of something better that will never eventuate due to inaction.

News flash! No one is going to show up on your doorstep and hand you everything you've ever wanted. If you are to achieve the things you want, you have to work hard towards them. Work out what you can do today, right now, to take a small step towards achieving whatever it is you want the most. Then another, and so on.

To me, true freedom is travelling, going where I want to go, doing what I want to be doing, living in the moment. In 2014, I travelled through Europe prior to coming to prison later that year. I loved every minute of that trip. I had the time of my life. Those memories and the feeling of freedom I experienced has sustained me through some very shitty times in here. It opened my mind to the realisation that the world is a big, diverse, and wonderful place that is so much more than the little world I had been living in, mainly in Sydney, with the odd trip to the gold coast in Queensland.

I'd previously holidayed on Hamilton Island, Bali, and Singapore. I also spent 6 months based in Darwin while in the military. While not been completely confined to my little corner of the world, blind, and oblivious, this trip was something else in comparison. It mentally opened up the world for me. I can't wait to go out and explore more of it. I've mentioned travelling in this section of the book, because living in the now provides such a sense of freedom – from regrets of the past along with the fears and stress of the future. Travelling was when I felt this sense of freedom and 'nowness' the most.

I mentioned a few pages ago about marketing companies making us feel shit to sell us rubbish. Well, rather than succumbing to their tactics and spending money on expensive shit like designer clothes, a Mercedes, latest iPhone, or just partying every weekend, whatever it is you find yourself wasting money on to feel better, put that money aside, go travelling, and enrich your life seeing some of the world.

To answer my own earlier question: 'What does success look like to me?' Success is true freedom: being free to be happy, free to pursue the things I want and choose for myself, free to work on achieving my goals, free financially, free of prison and the issues that landed me here, free to live my life with those I care about, free to explore the world. Success to me is not the accumulation of wealth or possessions.

There should be no negative connotations associated with success here. I have things I want to achieve. I'm goal-orientated and future-focused, which in the context of the poem's topic 'The Time Is Now' may seem quite contradictory, yet it is anything but. I hope to be successful in my endeavours – my version of success, not by others' measure but my own.

The point to make here is that my happiness is not dependent on reaching those targets. I'm happy today working towards them and enjoying the process. Happiness should not depend on future circumstances being met. If it takes 10 years to get there, you'll be miserable and dissatisfied for an entire fucking decade. If your goal was to lose 20 kilos, taking action by exercising daily and keeping a clean, healthy diet, and feeling better along the way should be source of satisfaction. You're on your way. That's something to be happy about today, and if it makes you happy today, it will tomorrow as well. Keep going. This is a good source of motivation. However, if you were to look at it from the viewpoint of 'I will be happy when I lose the 20 kilos,' you'll not enjoy any sense of satisfaction until the goal is met, which will be demotivating, and it's likely you won't stick it out. It's the same goal viewed from two different states of mind – one is conducive for success, the other for failure.

One of the greatest things I've discovered while in prison is the benefits of meditation. I will drop a disclaimer right here that I am a complete novice with meditation. I just do what I think is correct from what I've read. What I'm doing feels right to me. I feel much less stressed, more relaxed in general, happier, and in such a better place mentally after meditating. To be able to say that from prison speaks volumes. It works.

Most simply, the basic premise of meditation aims to clear the mind of thought, relax, and be present in the moment. Meditation has its role in the concept of living in the now. I highly recommend learning a bit about it and incorporating it into your routine. A lot of very successful, high-achieving individuals use meditation as a tool. Athletes, business elite, entrepreneurs, famous actors and musicians, academics, and world leaders all use meditation to help them focus and perform at the high levels required to do what they do. If meditation can be effective for them, imagine what it has the potential to do for you too. Why not give it a go? If it simply helps you to feel a little less stressed and nothing more. Isn't that alone worth the small effort?

Find a few reasons to be happy and grateful for what's good in your life right now. Accept the past, and make peace with it. Don't worry about the future. Worrying won't help one bit. Get going on living the life you want to live today. Take action. There is no better time than now.

'There is no way to happiness, happiness is the way.'

—Thich Nhat Hanh

Vietnamese Buddhist monk, author, peace activist, teacher, poet.

The Time Is Now

You can't revisit the past,
Nor can any of us travel forward in time.
The only place you'll ever be
Is right now this present moment of life.

Yesterday is long gone.
What is there to gain from what cannot be changed.
Let go of it,
For wishing things were different is only wishing in vain.

Tomorrow is not promised.
To live for something better that is faraway
Is not living at all.
The only time to experience this life is today.

There is certainly no wrong
In planning for the future; in fact, it's the smart move,
But to seek happiness later,
Is only setting yourself up to lose.

Planning for the future
Is an action made in the present day.
Set goals and dreams.
Take the first step; set off on that journey today.

The time is now
to live your life; where else could you be.
The past has past,
that's a fact, and the future is not guaranteed.

Find happiness and satisfaction
in what you have and what's good right now.
Just to be alive,
a healthy human being; you could have been born a cow.

Recidivism

Recidivism simply refers to individuals who reoffend and often return to prison. In my experience – and this is backed up by the statistics – the majority of people who serve time in prison will return at some point. During my time incarcerated, I often witnessed people come in and out of custody multiple times. I too have found myself in gaol on three occasions. Most recidivists will return to gaol for the same type of offences, usually stemming from the same unresolved issues.

An example of this might be repeat drink driving offences caused by unresolved alcoholism. Another common repeat offence is breaking and entering to support a drug addiction. Again and again, the same individuals commit the same offences, because they never addressed the root cause of the offending behaviour while in prison.

It's understandable that the wider community and especially victims of any crime are angry at the fact that criminals continue to reoffend, feeling as though they are being let down by a system that should be protecting them. How right you are to feel this way.

A common view held by regular citizens, which I hear frequently from talk back radio personalities and social commentators, etc., is that we should impose tougher sentences and make conditions in prison harder, many thinking prisoners have it too easy. People think judges are too soft, and the guidelines they sentence by are inadequate.

People are angry, because they are scared. They are entitled to be. After all, there is no such thing as a victimless crime. Each time a recidivist commits an offence, more people have to suffer as a result. This is just the reality of it. No two ways about it. Public anger with this issue is understandable and warranted. The call to get tougher on offenders seems a fair response.

I am going to ask that we put our anger aside for a moment to consider and alternate viewpoint.

In 1989, what was known as 'truth in sentencing' was introduced in New South Wales with the '1989 sentencing act' and endorsed by the Australian Law Reform Commission. The legislation removed any chance of prisoners having time taken off their sentence for good behaviour and efforts made to rehabilitate. The legislation ensured inmates would serve the full non-parole period of their sentence.

Those in opposition to the bill argued that to remove any incentive for inmates to rehabilitate would be counter-intuitive to the purpose of them being in prison, but the bill was popular and passed. Many state and federal politicians run election campaigns with a hard-line approach on crime and reform. It's an effective strategy, and they often win. As a result, over the past few decades, sentences for most offences have increased on average, while police are given more and more powers to put criminals away with ever growing budgets. Happy days, right?

Ask yourself this. During this time, have you noticed any reduction in crime?

That, after all, should be the consequence of effective policy, law reform, and billions of dollars spent on expanding policing capabilities and locking people away for extended periods of time. That's what we are all lead to believe when we vote for these politician's vowing to clean it all up.

I think the general public would expect that when an offender is incarcerated, corrective services and those employed within the corrective system would make every effort to rehabilitate the inmate to prevent them from committing further offences once released. That should be the objective. It is after all named corrective services for that fucking purpose.

Ideally, inmates while in custody would address their offending behaviours, rehabilitate, and reintegrate back into society, breaking the cycle of recidivism.

I assure you, this does not happen.

At the time of writing, the current rate of recidivism in New South Wales, those returning to prison within two years of release is 51.5%, with 58.7% returning to some sort of corrective services management, meaning some who reoffend might receive the equivalent of a good behaviour bond, community service, etc. Those figures are just within two years of release.

Almost 6 out 10 people will reoffend within two years!

I will add that there are programs available in prison that do address drug and alcohol addiction, violent offending, and other programs. The problem is they are hard to get into, as they are run at a limited number of prisons with limited spots. Inmates who want to participate are often not eligible, because certain criteria must be met to qualify. After having participated in these courses during this current sentence for the first time (during my previous two sentences, I was not eligible during three years of incarceration at that point or for the first two years of this sentence), I can see why they are largely ineffective.

The corrective system is set up to punish, not rehabilitate. In May 2016, the then-corrective services minister David Elliott and corrective services commissioner Peter Severin announced the Better Prisons Initiative, drastically reducing the budget for education services within New South Wales prisons, due to which 130 qualified teaching positions were made redundant. I mean, why would anyone want prisoners to educate themselves and gain skills to help them gain meaningful employment upon release?

With the removal of incentive with the truth in sentencing legislation, along with the lack of opportunity for education and offending addressing courses available, is it any wonder the statistics read the way they do? This is in addition to the toxic, violent drug culture that exists in the prison system. People get worse in prison, not better.

This view that exists of making sentencing and conditions in prison harsher comes from a place of fear and anger. How often do good decisions and outcomes result from this state of mind?

If you treat someone like an animal for long enough, they very likely act like one. Ask yourself this. Do you really want more angry, violent, and drug-addicted animals on the street being released from prison? This is what the current prison system often produces. Over 99.99% of people in prison will be released at some point, so you can save your 'lock them up and throw away the key' rhetoric, Alan Jones. It's never going to happen. They don't hand out life sentences for break and enter offences, drug offences, violence, or any offence other than murder, heinous sex offences, and large drug importation. Nor should they.

The average length of custodial sentence in New South Wales at the time of writing is ten months as per the Bureau of Criminal Statistics and Research. Shouldn't that average of ten months be used to make every effort to get that person on the right path from the moment they come into contact with the system? Shouldn't programs be available from day one to address the kind of offence they are accused of? What about incentivizing and rewarding participation in such courses along with good behaviour in custody, rather than our current almost purely punitive approach, which I can say from my own experience and observation does not work.

Change within the corrective and justice system as a whole is needed, with a shift towards rehabilitation and a view to help people overcome the issues that are causal to offending in the first place. The view should be to intervene at the earliest interaction with the corrective system and actually view the corrective system as it is so named to be – a corrective and rehabilitative system. As it exists today, I suggest it be renamed punitive services or criminal enhancement services. Not only should offence addressing courses be readily available but also education services to help inmates gain skills, qualifications, and experience they can take into the community to gain meaningful employment and succeed, in addition to an effective pathway support network to assist released offenders into employment and services.

I suggest the reason that this is not the case is this. If those employed within the correctives system actually implemented effective measures to tackle the recidivism issue, their jobs would be under threat through lack of necessity. With fewer repeat customers coming back through the revolving door, the prison population would shrink, and fewer positions would be required. Prisons are absolutely a business. To think of them as anything other than such is just plain ignorance. Why else would private companies such as Serco and MTC own and run them in the first place? Prisons are big business. CSI (Corrective Services Industries) is a commercial company that makes hundreds of millions of dollars profit each year. To reduce the prison population would greatly affect the bottom line, which is dependent on extremely cheap labour. Much like the American economy was built on the slaves' back, CSI uses almost non-existent labour costs, paying inmates $20–30 per week in wages to prop up huge profit margins. To reduce recidivism rates and prisoner numbers would be reducing their workforce and therefore their greatest profit-making commodity. No successful business will ever take a course of action that would detrimentally affect their ability to continue raking in massive profits. This is the true reason the recidivism issue never improves and crime rates remain stagnant. Too many people profit from the current status quo – police, lawyers, judges, anyone employed within the prison system, CSI, and any company benefitting from doing business with them are all enjoying jobs and profit from things remaining the same. Crime is an economic driver. Crazy but true.

Breaking the cycle of recidivism will take a new way of thinking that to many would be unpopular. It will probably cost votes to whoever suggests it and will cost money. Until we are able to make this shift towards a new way of thinking and invest in the revolving door that is our prison system, it will keep spinning. Things will continue in the same way they always have. Those same talk back radio show hosts and their listeners will have plenty to complain about as they continue to be the victims of these repeat offending criminals who are likely to never change.

To quote Charlie Sheen, #winning!

> 'The purpose of life is a life of purpose.'
>
> —Robert Byrne

Recidivism

The same faces again,
I've seen you here many times before.
What happened this time,
The same old problems landing me in prison once more.

For some familiar faces,
Prison is just a second home.
It's just a part of life.
In and out is all they have ever known.

Although I too have reoffended,
I can't understand this state of mind.
I could never accept
This horrible place as any home of mine.

It really makes me wonder
What kind of life they have outside.
How shit things must be
To be comfortable with constantly coming back inside.

It's easy to take the view
To make prisoners life hard while in gaol.
Punish, punish, punish,
But in solving crime, it's to no avail.

There is no rehabilitation
To be found inside of gaol walls.
So when someone reoffends,
Their next victim might just be you or yours.

The system is a failure.
Have you noticed any fall in crime?
Hundreds of years punishing,
still the same people return time after time.

It's time for something new.
Let's think outside the box; let's get crazy,
and actually try to solve this problem,
because everyone running the system is too fucking lazy.

When Your Number's Up

How old will you be when you die? How long do you have left? It is going to happen, after all. It is an absolute certainty. These are not questions that we often consider; maybe we should. It can be confronting contemplating our own inevitable death. It is one of those topics that is usually comfortably out of sight out of mind. Just ignore it, and it will go away. Sorry, but it won't.

From having had multiple close brushes with death myself, along with having had some close to me die young, it has made me think a bit deeper about my own mortality and death in general more than the average person. I survived being shot in 2018; several other bullets missing me by inches. In 2016, I was badly burnt in a fire that killed my best friend. Also in 2016, another friend was murdered, shot multiple times in an execution killing. I've also had other friends survive attempts on their lives. Amongst the group of people I grew up around and associated with well into my twenties, many are no longer with us, and most are either in prison for serious offences or have served their time. Even as teenagers, violence was common, with multiple incidents occurring and several charged with murder as juveniles. All of it has given me a perspective on death that I couldn't have gained without those experiences.

Often, when people have experiences with death through a close call of some kind, a cancer scare, or a loved one passing, it can jolt us awake and force us to consider our mortality. We may assess our choices, our priorities, our shortcomings. It provides us the opportunity for new perspective.

Let's consider a smoker with a 30-year habit who is now confronted with a cancer diagnosis. Every day of those 30 years, our smoker is aware of the harm their smoking is causing, increasing the risk of developing illness and disease, knowing full well it may kill them. Yet, with the 'out of sight, out of mind' approach to death, they puff away on those little death sticks, obliviously until the day they are confronted with the consequences. Suddenly, those 30 years of ignorant bliss become blindingly obvious stupidity. Having known many smokers who have developed cancer, I can say that all of them have quit upon receiving their diagnosis. Isn't that madness! Everyone just assumes themselves to be among the lucky ones who haven't or won't develop the disease, until they hear the dreaded news. Rather than take the tough option while they are still healthy and battle the addiction, they take the easy option and continue with it until they are forced to battle the addiction and cancer together.

Ignorance is not bliss, it is just plain ignorance.

Another example is surviving a car accident. One day, you're minding your own business driving along a road, doing nothing wrong, when boom! An out of control car ploughs into you. Just like that, when you least expect it, in a single moment, everything can change. This happens every single day. Yet, we drive around blissfully ignorant to the dangers of driving on the road. Like our smoker, we believe ourselves to be among the lucky ones, because it hasn't happened to us. Unfortunately, some don't survive that accident. For those that do, that's a brush with death. How would you feel in that situation?

For me, when I think about those close calls, I ask myself, would I have been satisfied with the life I have lived up until that point, had I died on those occasions? The answer is a resounding, 'Fuck no!' Not at all. I would be very disappointed if that was it for me. I know I could've done so much better. When that inevitable day does come, I want to be able to look back upon my life with satisfaction and say I lived a good life and that I'm happy with how I played my hand.

The issue is that I obviously don't know when that day will come. How long do I have to turn it around? One year, two, eighty? All of a sudden, I feel a sense of urgency. I have so much I want to achieve, and I may only have a short period of time in which to do it. This motivation is the benefit of contemplating mortality, along with the appreciation for the fragility of life itself adding valuable perspective.

Once you realise that your time on earth is precious and fleeting, you naturally ask yourself some big questions. 'How am I going to best use my valuable time in the most productive and meaningful way? Am I living my best life? Do I need to reassess my priorities?' And the question I asked myself: 'Would I be satisfied if I died?'

How could assessing your life situation, goals, and priorities in this way not bring about positive change in your life? How could it not bring about a positive shift in your thinking and help you focus on what is important?

Yes, it can be daunting to contemplate your clock ticking down to zero. But can you imagine how much worse it would feel laying on your death bed, looking back on your life with regret? Knowing you're out of time? Feeling as though you've wasted your life, not achieving the things you would've liked to? Not having lived the way you wanted? All because you had your head in the sand ignoring the fact that your time is finite.

What I know for sure is that our time on earth is precious and fleeting. Any day can be our last. No one wakes up thinking today could be their last. But one day, that day will come. It will not matter whether your prepared or not, nor will it matter what important plans your still to finalise.

Death does not care. When your numbers called, that's it. Your time is up.

With this perspective, I have made every effort to resolve the issues that have repeatedly landed me in prison. What a waste of life it is spending time in this shithole. I have set goals, and each day, I do whatever I am able to do to work towards achieving them. I will continue working hard while I am lucky enough to have this gift of life, because I know full well that it can all end any day.

Today, right now is the best time to start if you've got unfinished business. Act with a sense of urgency, focusing on working towards the things you want to achieve. Spend your precious time with the people most important to you, living your best life, and being the best version of yourself, enjoying each day along the way.

The clock is ticking down to the day when your time is up.

'The trouble is you think you have time.'

—Buddha

When Your Number's Up

None of us know
How many years we have on this earth.
Some people's flame burns long,
While others' light is just a burst.

This uncertainty makes life special,
Each day a wonderful gift to savour.
The fact our time is finite
Only adding more spice to life's flavour.

No matter your faith,
Regardless of the beliefs you may hold,
One thing that's universal to all,
When you are called, you go, young or old.

To worry is foolish,
For worrying cannot change the inevitable.
Your precious time is fleeting,
Make the best use of the time you have available.

Right now is the best time
To set goals and follow your dreams.
When your numbers up,
Finished or not, that's the end of your schemes.

I love my life,
The good and the bad, the full experience I'll know.
I hope I live one hundred years,
But when death calls, without fear I will go.

An Ode to Harley

Harley was my closest friend, best mate, my brother. Not by blood but by bond. He was a good man. As loyal a friend as you'll ever find. A loving father. He was honest (if he was thinking something, he would say it, regardless of the situation or how it may be taken). He lived by his morals and did things his own way. A free soul. He never missed the opportunity for a good time. Above all, just a genuinely good person who added value to anyone's life lucky enough to have him part of it.

I met Harley around 2011 on one of my regular trips to the gold coast of Queensland. Harley lived with a mutual friend who I had gone to high school with. It was while catching up with this school friend that I was introduced to Harley. My school friend, Harley, and I, along with a few others, met for drinks. After several drinks, we all got a bit loud and rowdy. I hate cigarette smoke. I can't be around it. I asked Harley, who was smoking, if he didn't mind holding the cigarette away from me and blowing the smoke it another direction, which he did, but over the course of the afternoon, he kept forgetting, and I kept asking him, which after a while really started to annoy me. After several more requests, I ended up telling him if I had to ask him one more time, I would put the cigarette out on his face. Sure enough, he forgot again, so true to my word, I took his cigarette and doused it on his forehead. Everyone was shocked, and a few words were exchanged between me and others of his group, but Harley thought the whole thing was hilarious. It threw me. I was thinking, 'I've just burnt this guy's face with a cigarette. I'm up on my feet ready for a fight, and he thinks it's funny.' He shook my hand and said, 'I like you. You're a man of your word.'

He later told me he was testing me to see what I would do. I guess I passed his test.

It's rare to have someone come into your life who has such a profound impact on it the way he did on mine. He showed me what it was to have and to be a true and loyal friend, someone who genuinely just enjoys your company, wanting nothing from you other than your friendship. Whether you had it all or were down to your last dollar mattered not one bit.

After a rocky start, we became close mates very quickly. We did a lot of partying, drinking, and drugs together. I tried to outdo his outrageous behaviour, and in return, his antics would upstage mine. I lived in Sydney but would fly up once or twice a month until I was arrested there on one of my trips. I was released on bail, with one of my bail conditions being I wasn't allowed to leave the state. Another was that I had to reside at Harley's address. Things really escalated from that point on. We went out nearly every night of the week. Harley had a girlfriend at the time who was not at all impressed with the situation. She hated me. After a few months, they broke up, which just meant more time for partying and nights out at the strip clubs. I also had a girlfriend and a young child back in Sydney, but I never let that fact get in the way of my wild partying ways.

Harley continued with his tests of my character. He once asked me to meet him at one of our favourite bars in Surfers Paradise, so I did. After waiting and a few drinks later, he showed up. He walked over to the table I was sitting at and pulled a small bag from his pocket containing two tablets. He said that I couldn't ask any questions, I just had to take one and deal with it. So I did. I never asked what they were, and to this day, I have no idea what he gave me. Fuck! Did that tablet rock me. For those of you who have seen the movie *Wolf of Wall Street* with Leonardo Dicaprio, think of the scene when Jordan and his business partner Donnie (played by Jonah Hill) take the lemon quaaludes and lose all control of their motor functions. If you're familiar with the scene, you'll know how extremely fucked up they were. Well, that's kind of what happened to us after consuming these tablets. For those of you who haven't watched the movie, go watch it. It's a great film but will give you an idea of the terrible state I was in walking around Surfer's Paradise.

Harley would often say, 'This is why you're my best mate. Nobody else would ever go along with these things.' It gave him great joy that, no matter what, he had a friend that was with him 100%, no questions asked. Tragically, the last time I went along with him no questions asked, we did something very stupid, and it cost him his life. Harley died in 2016 aged just 29 years old.

Grief is extremely tough to go through. The emotional pain is so intense that the pain feels physical. Anyone who has ever lost someone close to them knows this feeling. Guilt is often attached to our grief, despite no blame whatsoever being able to be attributed for the death. In my case, however, I felt directly responsible. I was complicit in going along with a course of action that caused Harley's death. The police also took this view. I was charged with the manslaughter of my best friend, a man I love as a brother. While dealing with the most crushing grief I had ever experienced, laying in hospital for over six weeks recovering from my own significant injuries, the police came and charged me with manslaughter, and I was sent to prison. Talk about body blow on top of body blow. To say I felt low is a severe understatement. I hated myself more than I have ever hated anyone else in my life. I was angrier with myself then I had ever been with another person. I felt that way for a long time.

Harley's daughter was six months old when he passed away. She would grow up never knowing her father, never experiencing all those special moments every girl deserves to have with their dad. I couldn't get that thought out of my head. I couldn't deal with it. So I didn't. I've talked about drugs and the availability of them in prison. I buried my grief, self-loathing, problems, pain, shame, and all the other shit under multiple drug habits at once. For almost a year, I refused to deal with any of it and used drugs every day, not to feel better but not to feel anything at all. I didn't want to think about any of it. I didn't want to think about anything at all, period.

I became addicted to Xanax, a heavy-duty prescription anti-anxiety medication, and buprenorphine, also a prescription drug to treat heroin addiction. It's basically a synthetic opioid with similar effects but to a much lesser extent.

Eventually, I decided that I couldn't go on like this, not dealing with things. I knew I had to confront the pain and start dealing with everything that had happened. Step one was kicking the drug habits. I went cold turkey, kicking both at the same time. I felt as though I would die for the first week or so. The withdrawal symptoms were severe. Apparently, Xanax and alcohol withdrawals are the only two that can actually kill you going cold turkey. Well, I can tell you, I felt as though I came close, but I was determined to stick it out. Making matters worse, there was an abundance of both the drugs I was withdrawing from available in my unit. My two cellmates had plenty and were both using the drugs in my presence and offering them to me regularly. The will power it took in that situation, feeling as close to death as I did to resist the easy option, and sticking it out is a strength I will draw on for the rest of my life.

I felt terrible for over a month. It was around six weeks before I started to feel myself again and about that long until I could sleep a full night. That ordeal was step one of a long road to dealing with everything. Let me tell you that it's impossible to do anything constructive with your life when you're a drug-fucked mess. I'm not going to sugar-coat my message or moderate my speech. If you want to effectively address any issue, being honest and direct is the only way to go about it. Acknowledging the fact that I was a mess was the first step in being able to sort it out. If your drug-fucked, you'll be no good to anyone else or to yourself until you sort yourself out. If you're obese, lazy, a problem gambler, a shit parent, or any one of a thousand other ways we fall short of the mark, the only way to ever improve ourselves and do better is to be honest with ourselves about it.

During my comedown period towards the end of 2017, the charge of manslaughter against me was dropped. In the eyes of the law, I had no legal responsibility for Harley's death. But I didn't feel any less responsible. I didn't care what the law or some judge or prosecutors' opinion was. I felt just as guilty over it as I had all along. My legal battle may have been over, but my internal battle was only just beginning.

I remained in prison for another six months on other charges until my release in May 2018. Once released, the reality of Harley being gone bit hard. The bubble of prison had been insulating me from the reality of the outside world. This was even more the case due to the drug haze I had been in for a good portion of the sentence. For the first time, I found myself exposed to the real world consequences with no buffer. Again, I kept thinking about Harley's daughter and her mother who was raising her as a single parent. I was reliving the traumatic events of night he died. I felt more guilty than I ever had about the whole situation. I felt even worse for the fact that I had been in prison sheltered from the harsh ramifications of our stupidity, hiding under a drug habit, while everyone else had to face it all out in the real world every day. I wore the guilt and trauma heavily around my neck. Once again, I didn't deal with it in any constructive way. I lasted eight weeks before I picked up a bottle of Xanax, got drunk, committed another offence, and came straight back to prison.

I let down everyone who I had promised to be there for all over again – Harley's young daughter, her mum, Harley's own mother who had all supported and stood by me when all I felt I deserved was their hatred and blame. Here they were supporting me when they were all suffering their own grief, loss, and pain.

What a poor way to repay those amazing people by going back down the exact same path again, apparently having not learnt a thing, letting them down, along with my son and my own family, who had also supported me through everything. For this reason, I felt even worse than when Harley had died. I was letting him down all over again as well. My self-loathing and hatred for myself hit new highs, while I hit new emotional lows.

The positive side to this all-time low of crushing lows was that it made me more determined than I had ever been to sort my shit out. I had no idea how I was going to do it, but the desire to do it was strong. I would show everyone who had suffered so much as a result of my actions that their love and support was appreciated and not for nothing. I stayed away from the drugs this time, instead focusing my attention on working out how to constructively address my issues. One of the ways I was able to stay focused was through exercise, which you've read about in 'Jail Fit'.

Reading was another great discovery for me in prison. Being able to educate myself through reading has changed my life. Writing the poetry in this book, as I learnt life's lessons, has also been a saving grace. One of those important lessons was to let go of the past and forgive myself. The value of looking back is in learning the lessons from our experiences, both the good and bad, but to dwell on them and hold on to those feelings serves no purpose.

Making peace with yourself and the past can be a very difficult task. It certainly was for me. I even felt guilty over forgiving myself, which is a normal response. That pain that has been consuming you and living rent free in your head doesn't want to be evicted. There will be resistance to self-forgiveness, but if you ever want to be free of the pain of the past, then you must allow yourself forgiveness. Accept that the past cannot be changed, no matter how badly you may wish for it. Hating yourself for your past mistakes won't fix them. It is nothing but destructive. To move forward, to be a happy, healthy, and functioning human being, at some point, you need to just let it go. You will likely feel conflicted about moving forward, but what's the alternative? Staying miserable, hating yourself, abusing substances to feel better or not feel, stuck on the merry-go-round of self-loathing? Who does that benefit? You're no good to anyone in such a state. The past is gone. You can't change it. Learn what you can from it and move on. This is one of the valuable lessons I've managed to squeeze from this tragedy and subsequent fallout. No matter how tough a situation or how hard the adversity you suffer is to endure, there is always value to be gained from it.

I've also learnt something about the strength of character and compassion that people are capable of. For Harley's loved ones to show the love and support, compassion and forgiveness they have towards me through the most horrific of circumstances, while enduring their own immense emotional pain and suffering is a testament to the amazing quality of human beings they are. I'm blessed to have them in my life. Thank you for everything. I love you all.

> 'When friendship leaves us through death, we feel cheated in life. Life doesn't play fair, so I vow to win the game for both of us.'
>
> —Amy Hoover

An Ode to Harley

What a time we had together.
Although brief, your impact was profound.
Despite the short years,
My friend, we are forever bound.

Your life cut short,
Too soon from this world you departed.
I will find you in the next life.
Our friendship has only just started.

Your daughter is so like you,
She reminds us of you in every way.
We all miss you so much,
And think of you each and every day.

Those you left behind,
I promise I will always care for.
I will be there for them,
Just as I was the friend you were always there for.

You lived by morals,
A loyal friend and a man of conviction.
My memory of you
Standing proud, you truly are a vision.

Our days were wild,
Always doing things our own way.
We lived on our own terms.
I loved every minute of every single day.

Good at pissing people off,
You would have thought it was our focus.
We definitely had a knack ,
For making everyone fucking hate us.

Those in our circle,
They knew we meant no harm.
But to everybody else,
Our behaviour was cause for serious alarm.

A thousand fond memories,
I miss those days with you, my brother.
Until we meet again, rest well.
Once more, I look forward to us seeing one another.

The Sentence Falls

The day of sentencing is a big deal. It's the day you have been awaiting for a long time, often years. You feel as though everything is riding on the number the judge hands down, the whole course of the rest of your life depending on the result. Everyone is hoping for a favourable outcome, but nobody knows what the judge might do. Results can vary a lot for identical charges. It's like a lottery. Some hit the jackpot with a great result, while others lose big, and the stakes are high. When you're talking about years of your life, in some circumstances decades, the stakes don't get much higher. Lawyers often have no idea how things will go, so how could we. We cross our fingers and hope for the best.

On the morning of sentencing, you wake up (that's if you sleep), and the stress kicks in immediately. It's the first thing you think of: 'Today's the day.' As stressful as the day is, everyone looks forward to having sentencing done, just to finally know how long you have to go, regardless whether the result is good or bad. The uncertainty is a killer. Not knowing is definitely the worst part of being on remand, despite a thousand other shit things going on.

Going to court from gaol is such a shit process. Usually, the guards collect you from your cell at around 5–6 in the morning (in some prisons, it's earlier). You return anywhere from 6 pm to midnight. It's a fucking long day. Hours upon hours are spent in crowded holding cells. When being transported in the claustrophobic transport trucks, you'll be handcuffed. Hours upon hours more held in the courthouse holding cells, until finally, it's your turn to go before the judge, which may not be until late in the afternoon, giving you a lot of time with your racing thoughts. You could be in the courthouse holding cells with a dozen other inmates, but it's a very individual experience. One by one, each prisoner goes up to front the judge. Upon each man's return, everyone is asking how it went. Not because anyone gives a fuck about them at all, but to try to gauge what type of mood the judge is in. We want to know if this judge is in a heavy hitting mood or not. An angry judge on sentencing day is everyone's worst nightmare. It seems the longer the day goes on, the shorter their patience becomes. Based on this, everyone goes quietly back into their own thoughts, mulling everything over. People are pacing. Some are sitting staring blankly. Others are nervously tapping their feet. The tension in the room could be cut with a knife. Finally, you're called up, everyone wishing you luck. Again, not because they care, but maybe if you get some luck go your way, then they might too.

Courtrooms are open to the public. Anyone who wishes to sit in on any court proceeding can do so. If you feel like going and sitting in on a murder trial in the supreme court tomorrow, no one is going to stop you. My court cases have always attracted media interest, so along with random public that poke their heads in for a sticky beak, the gallery usually had plenty of reporters watching on as well.

Walking into the courtroom to see the judge, prosecutors, my defence team, police, sheriffs, court clerks, corrective services staff, media (jurors if at trial), and random strangers, all eyes focused on you, is an experience. I have had up to 200 people packed in like sardines to sit in on my matters. It's a whole other experience to get back to your cell, flick on the news, and watch a detailed report on the days court proceedings – your crime itself – and see several of the worst photographs of your head the reporters could dig up off the net. Then read all about it in the following day's *Telegraph*.

It's always comforting to look around the courtroom and see familiar faces smiling back at you. To have support is a big deal when there are plenty of people in the room who would gladly see you receive the death penalty, if it were an option.

The court process in a thorough one. Good luck if you're a private person and are embarrassed easily. Your life is about to be opened right up like a can of worms. They go into great detail about every aspect of your life (so long as it's relevant to the case). That includes your childhood and circumstances of your upbringing, detailed excerpts from psychology reports referencing past trauma, anxiety, and depression issues, drug and alcohol abuse, personal medical information, as well as in-depth details about the offence itself and what lead up to it. The court hears the prosecutor and defence discuss your mental state at the time, influencing factors, witnesses against you, victim's testimonies, all the while the prosecutor doing his best to absolutely rubbish you as a human being, and they are good at it. By the end of it all, the prosecutor had me convinced I was as big a piece of shit as Ivan Milat.

This is all laid bare before a courtroom full of strangers while media note it all down for tonight's news and tomorrow's papers.

But sitting in the dock, none of that matters. Fuck what all the strangers think, and screw the prosecutor and media. The only person in that court room whose opinion matters is the judge. All you care about is what the judge is thinking and saying, building towards handing down the sentence. By the point in the legal process when you are being sentenced, your guilt has already been determined. You would either have been found guilty at trial or plead guilty at an earlier stage. If you are taking the stand at sentencing, it's to show remorse, talk about what you have learnt from it, apologise, and express your commitment to rehabilitation and to not commit further offences. It goes in your favour to front up, own up to your mistakes, and show genuine remorse. The shittest part about this is that the prosecutor gets to pepper you with questions to test the authenticity of your testimony. They open you up like a can of worms and do their level best to fuck you up. It is their aim to make you look like the world's biggest lying piece of shit. They want to frustrate you into losing your cool, getting under your skin with insults to force a reaction showing that you're quick to anger.

They'll ask the same questions many different ways, looking for small differences. Any inconsistency they can attack, they will latch on to it and destroy your credibility. These are highly educated, intelligent people who are experienced practitioners plying their trade against often uneducated crooks. The experience is a real test of your character. It's not easy to get through, and many people come undone on the stand. It's extreme pressure in a public arena with high stakes. Years of your life can depend on how well you stand up to it. It's not a situation in which you want to come off second best.

After the judge has heard both the prosecution and defence submissions, he or she will sum everything up in detail, after which the offender will be asked to stand for judgement. The sentence is then handed down as such:

(This is verbatim from my own sentencing transcript)

> *Mr Keighran, you are convicted. I impose upon you an aggregate sentence of imprisonment with partial accumulation. That sentence comprises a total term of seven years three months imprisonment to expire on 16 October 2025. The non-parole period is one of four years three months and will expire 16 October 2022.*

After that, the judge just stands up and walks out.

As the judge walks out, you are handcuffed by the corrective services staff, who walk you back down to the holding cells while you're frantically doing the math in your head, working out how long is left until you can go home. At the time I was sentenced, I had two-and-a-half years remaining. Still with a while to serve at the time, I was relieved that the matter was dealt with and the uncertainty finally over.

I could set my sights on a fixed date. I had a timeline to attach my goals to and could start making plans with certainty. I was able to tell my son when Dad would be home.

From that point on, it's a long countdown to freedom.

'Freedom is the oxygen of the soul.'

—Mashe Dayan

The Sentence Falls

Almost two years I have waited
For the judge to hand down my fate.
I hope she shows mercy.
I have turned things around; I hope it's not too late.

My palms are sweating,
My stomach's in knots; in bed awake I lay.
Four o'clock in the morning,
I will know my sentence by the end of today.

The cell door opens early.
From the prison to court I must travel,
To be judged for my crime,
Standing before the court, the judge, and her gavel.

As proceedings begin,
I look around the gallery to see its full of strangers.
Media take their notes,
While unknown public listen as the judge details my failures.

I spot my family.
They smile to show their support.
I smile back,
Letting them know I'm fine exposed before the court.

I take the stand
To say my piece; I have genuine remorse.
I have worked through the issues
That led me here; I'm sorry it had to run its course.

I'm asked to stand
To hear my fate, as the sentence falls.
She speaks of years as if nothing.
Does she know what life is like behind jail walls?

I accept the punishment,
Returning to prison with the number in my head.
I'm just relieved it's over,
Finally knowing how far this road is ahead.

The countdown to freedom begins,
Like a race with the finish line in view.
Although some way off in the distance,
I see a new life waiting for me that is long overdue.

Prison Politics

Politics is a big deal in prison. It is complex but once understood becomes clear and simple. There is a lot to explain here, so I will break it all down and try simplify it.

Some offences are just not acceptable to the general prisoner population, which may come as a surprise to people. An example of this would be any sexual offence. Sex offenders are not tolerated in the main, and a standing attack-on-sight policy applies. These offenders are usually separated from the general prison population. Anyone who comes across one of these sex offenders and doesn't deal with them in the expected way may become a target themselves. Sex offenders are despised in the prison system. For this reason, sex offenders are usually housed in the protection units, or the boneyard, as we call it.

People who cooperate with the police – police informants, assist with investigations, write statements, testify in court, set someone up to be arrested, snitches – are all just known as dogs.

The worst thing you can be labelled as in prison is a dog. There is also an attack-on-sight policy for dogs. People who go down this path of becoming a dog usually do so for a reduction in sentence for their cooperation. Police and prosecutors will support them in court receiving a discount and do their best to encourage someone who's been charged with an offence to give information on either other's that are involved in their crime or other crimes altogether.

To be called a dog in prison is a very serious accusation. If someone calls you a dog, you must fight him immediately. If not, it will be assumed that you are guilty of being one.

On the flip side of that situation, If you were to accuse someone of being a dog, you would want to be able to back that claim up with evidence and produce the proof in support of it. If not, there's a good chance you will become a target yourself.

Prison is very race orientated. Religion also plays a part, mainly with the Muslim inmates. The koori (aboriginal) inmates stick together, the Asians stick with the Asians, the Lebo's together, who are predominantly Muslim. Then there are the Islander gangs which are at war with each other but back each other against other groups.

Generally, if someone has an issue with one of the Asians, for instance, then the other Asians will all back up their guy. Let's say, for example, that an Aussie is accusing a particular Asian inmate of being a dog, if the Aussie produces proof in the form of paperwork (a police statement or court transcript), then prison politics protocol is that the dog has to get beaten up and sent to the boneyard. It would generally be up to the Asians to deal with themselves (in-house) to a standard that is acceptable to the rest of the prison population. One or two punches wouldn't meet that standard at all; he would need to cop a severe beating. If this doesn't happen, others will step in to do a proper job of it. If the Asians were to try and prevent this from happening, then that is how race wars kick off, which can get very ugly. This sort of shit happens all the time.

Drug use is rampant in prison, and a lot of trouble stems from it. Most trouble in here is related to people not being able to pay their drug debts. Despite usually being clear that debts are due on time, this doesn't always happen. Drug addicts will say and agree to just about anything, promising the world and committing to paying an amount by a certain time that they know they are very unlikely to be able to honour.

All that matters while they are hanging out is getting the drugs to make the suffering stop. The consequences are secondary and something to be dealt with later… or not even a consideration at all.

The people bringing the drugs into the prison are expected to look after their own kind (i.e., his own race, gang, religious group, etc.) with some drugs for free. If this doesn't happen, he is seen to be 'holding out' and may have issues within his own camp. A lot of internal fighting goes on over this type of thing. It's generally kept quiet, but black eyes are hard to hide. Everyone knows what's going on. Not much happens in prison that the whole population doesn't find out about pretty fast.

Inmates who appear to be too friendly with the screws (guards) can also run into trouble. As inmates, we rely on the screws to do all sorts of shit for us, starting from having phone numbers put onto our phone accounts so we are able to contact family and friends. Speaking to a welfare officer has to be organised through them. Finding out how much money is in our gaol account, getting more greens (clothes), getting an inmate request form, finding out our next court appearance date, and myriad other information or help we need with things, we have to ask the screws. That is not an accident. This is a deliberate ploy to make us as inmates completely dependent on them for anything we need done as a control tool. Obviously, they want complete control over the prison population, and having us dependent on them for what we want and need is an effective method for maintaining that control. The problem here for inmates is that if someone is seen to be speaking to the screws too frequently, it can raise suspicion that they may be snitching or just generally getting too friendly with them.

Another issue that can arise is someone 'talking out of school' about someone or something that they have no business speaking about. This is very much dependent on your standing in the pecking order. Someone higher up the food chain may speak ill of another inmate whom he considers to be a nobody. However, if someone else were to make those same comments, it may be seen as speaking out of school. Another example of this may be a member of a gang or crew speaking about others in their own camp, but if someone outside of that group were to make the same comments, they would be in big trouble.

Keeping your word in prison is everything. It's all you have. We are all in the shittest place imaginable with fucking nothing. Your word and standing up to it is your measure as a man. To say you will do something or can do something and not following through on it or going back on your word is not acceptable. It proves to everyone that you are not to be trusted. Not being trustworthy leads to suspicion, and if you find yourself under suspicion, your days are likely numbered.

You definitely don't want to let anyone bully, talk shit, or insult you. If you're seen as weak in any way, you're not likely to last long.

It doesn't matter who you are, how big, tough, or gangster you think you are, at some point, someone is going to pick you. It's easy to put on a tough guy act and get away with it out in society, but in here, you'll be found out pretty quickly if you're not up to the task. You will be tested.

As you can see, politics is complicated, but it all serves a purpose. No one wants to live with sex offenders. They tragically ruin the lives of their victims. They deserve whatever violence and retribution comes their way. Many inmates are in prison in the first place because an informant has snitched on them. No one wants to live with a dog. Don't snitch thinking you'll be putting yourself in a better legal situation. You may do less prison time, but the reduced time you do end up doing will be a nightmare. Everyone inside will want to kill you, despite having nothing to do with the case. It is an obligation to fuck you up for anyone who can get to you. When you find yourself in prison, whether you like it or not, this is home for a while, with the other inmates in your unit being your housemates. Living with others can be difficult at the best of times. Prison is a whole other level of complicated. The politics that govern in here are a form of keeping the peace and essentially laws/rules for an otherwise lawless group of individuals who largely choose to live outside the confines of society's laws. Everyone soon learns the expectations upon them and the consequences for indiscretions.

> 'Worry is like a rocking chair; it gives you something to do but never gets you anywhere.'
>
> —Erma Bombeck

Prison Politics

A different set of rules
Govern the population here in prison.
A democracy of the people
Held and enforced like a military division.

Learn the system quickly,
As there's little leeway for the uninitiated.
The smallest indiscretion
Can see you violently and publicly humiliated.

The guards have no say.
Inmates call the shots, ruling with iron fists.
Until you learn the ropes,
Tread carefully to keep yourself off the hit list.

People die in gaol.
This place is certainly not a joke.
It can be a warzone.
I suggest being wary of whose anger you evoke.

The rules have purpose,
And once understood it becomes clear why.
Certain things aren't tolerated
In this subculture where the law's eye for an eye.

Never call anyone dog.
Don't give people up or cooperate with police.
Don't commit sexual crimes.
Indiscretions landing you in hospital at the least.

Being repeatedly stabbed,
Kicked and have someone jump on your head,
This is the punishment inflicted.
For breaching these principles, some end up dead.

Many others apply.
The list of rules is complex and long.
Harsh as it may seem,
It makes living in here easier to get along.

Prison is the last place
The average person would expect political administration.
This self-regulating society
Where the lawless command the prison population.

Self-Destruction

At some point, we have all made bad decisions, acting in some way that is not in our own best interest: perhaps staying in a bad relationship, mixing with the wrong crowd, spending beyond our means, racking up bad debt, using drugs, drinking excessively, keeping a poor diet, and a thousand other poor choices people regularly make. These are all fairly standard behaviours that most of us are guilty of engaging in at some point or another. Many will be able to make a claim to all of the above. I can.

We make mistakes and learn from them. It's just a part of growing up, growing as a person, normal self-development, life.

But not for everyone. Some take things to the extreme. When something is not working out for them, rather than making an effort to correct the issue, moderate their behaviour, and learn, they will double down and continue engaging in risky behaviours, making poor choices, and ignoring warning signs, only making things worse for themselves. Often knowing full well the damage being caused, they either don't care or refuse to accept the reality of the situation. Despite their apparent ignorance, they're aware.

I know that, in my own experience, I have made a conscious decision at times to continue on behaving in a way that was causing me problems. In fact, I felt a certain freedom in throwing caution to the wind, running with the problem, even embracing it, rather than making the tough choice to stop and confront it. Allowing ourselves to fall further down the rabbit hole feels like the easy option at the time; to continue down rather than making the arduous climb out of it. In reality, this is only making things harder when that time does come to do it. To continue is the weak option.

To use another *Alice in Wonderland* analogy, at some point, you're going to have to face up to the monster (the jabberwocky) and get out of wonderland and back to the real world. For those who are not familiar with Lewis carol's *Alice in Wonderland*, Alice is terrified at the prospect of having to face the jabberwocky, a vicious three-headed, fire-breathing dragon. Alice is full of doubt. It seems a hopelessly impossible task for her to defeat the beast. I feel like this is the perfect analogy in dealing with the big issues that are causing problems or harm in our lives, as the task can feel this way.

It's easier to palm the issue away, run from it, make excuses, put off dealing with it until a later date, or ignore it all together, denying its existence. We defend ourselves when criticised about our choices, poor behaviour, habits, etc. We minimise the problem, go on the attack in response, deflect, and change the subject using whatever tactics we have at our disposal to fend of the attack. It's common to feel attacked when someone raises their concern about what's going on with us. More often than not, the concerned party is someone close to us raising the subject out of genuine care, worry, and compassion. Yet, we will harshly defend our position, inflicting pain with our words to warn them off.

All of this is destructive. The problems only get bigger and harder to deal with the longer it goes on. The consequences become more severe, and often, hitting rock bottom is the only way the fall ends.

That rock bottom may be a drug overdose, financial ruin, divorce, prison, mental breakdown, or death. All very confronting outcomes but an absolute reality. These are outcomes that we are aware of as a possibility but largely choose to ignore. I seriously doubt that someone who has several maxed-out credit cards, spending well beyond their means without sufficient income to pay them down, is unaware that their behaviour is unsustainable. They know full well that at some point, the debt must be paid. Unless they address the issue, stop spending, and seek help, it's unlikely they will ever be able to repay the debt, and the potential of financial ruin looms.

Drug addicts know that serious health issues and death through overdose is a possibility. People who engage in illegal activities know that prison is a real possibility. If you gamble your life savings away, not only is financial ruin almost guaranteed, there is a very high probability your wife, husband, or partner won't stick around when they realise you've lost everything. Yet, these types of behaviours are common, and the consequences are just as commonly ignored.

But when we experience that inevitable crash with the cold hard floor at rock bottom, the reality of those consequences of your actions can be crippling. Trust me, I've been in that dark place a few times. When you are finally forced to confront the beast from which you've been running, it is a scary and humbling experience. For some, it takes multiple rock bottom experiences before taking action towards addressing the issue, while others will never change.

To the average person, this seems like madness, and it is. It's easy to say, 'Well, just stop if you know something's an issue and sort it out.' For most, that's what they do; some take longer than others, but generally, that's what happens. For some, they just don't seem to be able to. The solution seems so simple from the outsider's perspective, but for the person going through it at the time, it can be anything but easy. At some point, they are going to have to make the hard choice or hit rock bottom.

We all have a choice, I don't care what excuses people come up with. Every day, in each moment, we can choose to make changes.

At any time, we can take a course of action to improve, make a correction, or stop what we are doing. You can either have your shitty excuses, or you can have success, but you can't have both.

For me, I had multiple rock bottom moments with severe consequences. Coming to prison for the first time does not even count as one of them. It didn't even register as a wake-up call. If you're not ready to change, you won't. Although I wasn't aware of it at the time, that was a choice I was making through my own arrogance and ego. It was a long and steep learning curve before I was able to recognise it. Chances are, if there was a flashing sign right in front of me saying, 'This is a massive problem. It's time to make some changes,' I wouldn't have noticed it. And that is exactly what it was. But I had a long way to fall from there before I hit my first rock bottom.

Looking back, there were so many warning sign events that would've been rock bottom moments for the average person. For me, they didn't even register. If only I had noticed those warning signs that were there flashing right in front of me for so long, I could've saved myself and many, many others a lot of pain and suffering.

When I eventually did take notice and make that tough choice to sort my shit out, working out how I was going to make the necessary corrections was a whole other issue. Trust me when I say, there is no help to be found in prison for guys who want make positive changes. A lot of people in that headspace have no idea how to actually implement the changes they want to make. They don't have the tools and know-how. The average citizen would expect there to be resources in prison to facilitate this rehabilitation, especially when someone reaches that point when they are ready and willing to do it, but this just isn't the case.

I had to work it out for myself, which is probably another reason it took a few goes at it, fucking up a couple more times along the way. But the knowledge, growth, self-development, and experience I've gained through the process has led me to this point where I can very confidently speak with authority on all the subjects I discuss through the book. I am now in a position to share it and hopefully help those who are experiencing their own battles. I've been there, done it, and overcome it. I didn't learn this shit in a book from some academic wanker who has never been down in the dark, shit places. I've walked many, many miles in these shoes and walked the hard roads. I'm not at all saying that you shouldn't listen to someone with an academic qualification; quite the opposite, you should 100% seek help to address issues that you are struggling with from a qualified professional. But if hearing the point of view of someone who has lived it first hand and learnt it all the hard way resonates with you more than those who have not, if that's going to break through and connect with you, setting you on that new path to a better, happier, healthier version of you, then I'm achieving my primary goal in writing this book.

It is all up to you. Make the choice to start that journey right fucking now! Or don't. It's your life. You can come up with more bullshit excuses, or you can have a great successful life, but you can't have both.

> *'Life presents many choices, the choices we make determine our future.'*
>
> —Catherine Pulsifer

Self-Destruction

Sometimes I feel like
There is freedom in being out of control.
Out of my mind,
Let loose on the world; look out, I'm volatile.

I never know when
I will get the urge to just let go,
But when I do,
How bad things might get, not even I know.

I love that feeling,
Throwing all caution to the wind.
Let's see where this goes,
By the end, I wonder the trouble I'll find myself in.

Why this is the case,
I'm still working out the reason.
My own worst enemy,
For crimes against my own interest, I
ought to be tried for treason.

Reverting to animal instinct,
It's time to drink, fight, and fuck.
Cocaine keeping me on my feet,
Out of the way, I'll run over you like a truck.

Is it a personality trait?
I've met others just like me.
Regardless, I won't let go again
Of this curse; I just want to be free.

Who would ever want
Anything other than to put their best foot forward.
To get ahead in life,
We strive to succeed moving onward and upward.

But when I push that button,
The one that says self-destruct,
No thoughts of self-preservation,
Like a volcano explodes when it erupts.

Recurring Dreams

I don't know much on the subject of dream interpretation. I don't know a lot about how the subconscious mind works. For the most part, I believe dreaming is our brain sorting out our thoughts and experiences, but occasionally, our subconscious mind is sending us a message through dream. I do my best to decipher the meaning behind my dreams, because I believe in the power of subconscious mind. I once sat up for hours one night in my cell trying to solve a jumbled word puzzle from the newspaper. I'm usually able to solve them without too much trouble, but this one had me stumped. I eventually went to sleep without having solved it. Upon waking up the following morning, the answer was immediately formed clearly in my mind. I got up and checked the answer against the spaces provided, double checking I had used all the letters. It was correct. The phrase fit. My subconscious mind had solved the puzzle and given me the answer while I slept.

I also think that there can be more to dreams than sorting out our thoughts, experiences, and solving the odd word puzzle. Twice in my life, I have had premonitory dreams come true in detail that couldn't possibly be coincidence.

In one of these dreams, I was driving along a street in my home town. I drove past a girl I had gone to high school with who was walking along the footpath, pushing a pram. That was the dream. When I woke up, I thought it was odd to dream about this girl, as I hadn't seen her for many years, and although we attended high school together, we weren't really close friends. We would say hello if we crossed paths, but that was it. We had different friendship groups and certainly weren't significant to each other in any way. Later that same day, I was driving, and I drove past the same girl I had dreamt of the night before, and she was pushing a pram, just as I had seen it in my dream. It blew my mind. I remember it clearly. I wasn't even aware that she had a child.

Although the dream and the event were something fairly innocuous, it had me in a spin. I had dreamt of a future event.

The second occasion was while I was travelling through Europe in 2014. I was flying into Amsterdam from Croatia or Spain I believe. I can't recall exactly, but we were to spend a few days partying in Amsterdam before heading to Belgium for a music festival. I was tired from all the travelling and partying, so I used the flight to catch up on some much needed sleep, and I doubted I would be getting much in Amsterdam. As I dozed, I had a vivid image, looking down to the ground below when a missile was fired up at the plane. I watched it snake its way through the air up closer and closer to the plane. It seemed as though it was going to hit us. Then right before impact, I woke up. I looked around; no one paid me any attention. I shrugged it off and went back to sleep.

After my short stay in Amsterdam, we travelled to Belgium for our music festival, where I was out of phone contact for a couple of days. The only place with a Wi-Fi signal was a small area of the camp ground with a tent erected and Wi-Fi station. I hadn't contacted home for a few days, as I was having too much fun, so I thought I had better head over and check in with the family. When I did, I found that my social media was full of messages from concerned family and friends asking where I was and if I was ok. Along with those messages, my news feed was full of news about Malaysian Airways flight MH17 being shot down. Flight MH17 took off from Amsterdam 17 July 2014, the same day I left Amsterdam to travel to Belgium. That flight was headed to Kuala Lumpur, nowhere near where I was travelling. I would never have been on that flight. I took the train from Amsterdam to Belgium, but my family didn't know that. All they knew was that I was in the country and leaving to head elsewhere.

I immediately remembered my dream. I believe what I saw was the shooting down of flight MH17, just the same as I saw in advance the girl from school walking with a pram. One was of no significance at all, and the other was a major world event. Make of all that what you will; I don't know what to make of it myself. I just know that what I dreamt in those two instances seemed very much to me to be a premonition in great detail of events that to me cannot be dismissed as mere coincidence.

Now, this monster in my dreams... a fucking T-Rex. I don't know what I've done to piss this thing off, but it hates me. It's not just hungry; it wants to fuck me up. It wants me dead and does not give up.

I'm sure there is some message in it that my subconscious mind wants me to understand. Unlike the word puzzle, there is no clear answer. This dream has reoccurred on and off for a couple of years, and there have been other times when the monster would change to a pack of wolves or a lynch mob. But it's the same deal, the same monster that wants to tear me apart. Mostly, it's in the form of this T-Rex. I'm obviously not getting the message, so my subconscious keeps sending it to me in the form of an angry fucking dinosaur.

The flying dreams started several years ago. My whole life, I have had dreams in which I'm running but can't get traction, essentially running suspended with my feet slightly off the ground. One night, I figured out in my dream state that if my feet are not on the ground, then I must be flying. I must be able to fly. I just spread my arms out wide, leant forward, and much like Peter Pan, I took flight in the same fashion.

Ever since then, I can fly in my dreams, although sometimes, I suddenly lose the ability and crash, while other times, I try but can't take off. This ability to take control of your dream in this way is called lucid dreaming. I've worked out that it was around the time I started meditation and reading about Buddhism when this ability awakened. I connected with the philosophy of it and have found the psychology quite helpful. After taking up meditation, I have found that I am calmer and happier in my general day-to-day life. There seems to be some correlation between all of it and the flying dreams.

As for the dreams about getting out of prison and finding myself in trouble again, this is clearly a fear of mine and something a lot of us worry about prior to our release. There is no message to be deciphered with this one. It's very common for guys and women who are released from custody to return after a short period of time, despite their best intentions. This is true in my own case, only lasting eight weeks before being arrested on new charges after my previous release.

A few years ago, I read a book by Dr Brian Weiss titled *Many Lives, Many Masters*. Dr. Weiss is a renowned psychiatrist. He uses hypnosis to treat people with psychological issues that conventional treatment methods are not able to get to the bottom of. During some hypnosis sessions, patients started to talk of past traumas that seemed to be from someone else's life. Before long, he came to the realisation that his patients were recounting past life experiences and even their own past deaths. Dr Weiss was able to verify one of his patient's death stories as she was able to give a detailed description of the event. She gave her past life name, date of death, the way she died (a car accident), and location. He was able to find an archived newspaper article from decades earlier matching her description.

This book was an amazing read, and I look forward to reading others he has written. It really made me contemplate the power of the subconscious mind, which is what is being tapped into during hypnosis.

Another aspect of this that he talks about is that sometimes our dreams are past life experiences. We may have a dream about a place we have never been, people we have never met, or another era in time in which we didn't live. I have experienced this myself. I dreamt I was a mariner in a harbour and was dressed in a soldier's uniform. I was in barracks with many others dressed the same way. There was some catastrophe, with a mast snapping and falling, sails and lines drowning men as the ship sank. We all ran from our barracks to the commotion. I boarded the ship to save whoever I was able to but died myself, drowning while attempting to save someone. The ships were old, wooden, colonial-looking things. From the ships and uniforms, I would guess the time period to be 17th or 18th century.

Whether or not I dreamt of a past death, I don't know. I believe I did. Due to my previously discussed premonitory dreams, what I have read in Dr Weiss' book, and what I feel to be true for myself, it seems to me there is something powerful about our subconscious mind and consciousness itself that we just don't understand. The earlier mentioned recurring dreams seems to be one of the ways my subconscious mind communicates with me. I will continue to try to understand the messages and meaning behind them, as I feel as though it's in my best interest. And I would very much appreciate if this T-Rex would fuck right off!

> *'When we are asleep in this world, we are awake in another.'*
>
> —Salvador Dali

Recurring Dreams

When the sandman visits
And sprinkles that dust over me,
Into another world I go,
A place of limitless possibility, a dream.

This other plane of existence,
Where the laws of physics don't apply.
I spread my arms,
Off I go; at will, I can take off and fly.

I soar high above all trouble,
As I look down peacefully upon the world.
Places I have known,
others new, lands with rivers of gold.

Another is not so pleasant,
my arch-nemesis in the world of dreams.
A place of nightmares,
where a relentless monster chases after me.

I run, I hide,
I do my best to avoid this angry foe.
Just when I have escaped,
Or think I have, my hiding spot is exposed.

Once or twice, he's got me,
But mostly, I manage to get away.
A ferocious adversary,
In the land of nod that will return another day.

Some have cryptic meaning,
While others, the message is clear.
I have another repeatedly
That exposes one of my greatest fears.

I'm set free of prison,
So happy to be back out in society.
Once again, I ruin it.
A wanted man, the long arm of the law is after me.

I wake in fright,
My body and mind tortured with stress.
Relief takes a moment.
I hope one day, I will finally put it all to rest.

Coming Back

Returning to prison is so much harder than coming in for the first time. Each subsequent time, coming back is worse still. At least that has been my experience. I'm sure most would agree with me. There are plenty of guys who return again and again who have become so accustomed to life behind bars, they see prison as a second home. For them, returning isn't so bad. The stress of trying to make their way in society is over. The simplicity of prison life is a welcome relief. These inmates have become institutionalised, and the recidivism cycle for them is likely to continue. However, for most of us, coming back in is tough.

    I experienced a deep depression and period of painful realisation when I came in for the third time to serve my current sentence. This poem is a reflection of that time.

    At the time I committed the offence which brought me back, I was serving a period of parole for a previous offence. Having only being released eight weeks prior, to return so soon was a big shock.

I am very lucky to have strong family support. I made a promise to them prior to my last release that I would not return to prison again. I had put them through enough hardship, having already gone through the whole process twice. I vowed to change my ways. I obviously broke that promise, for which I felt incredibly bad. I had let everyone down who suffered through the previous years without me at home. They supported me during that time, only to have me fuck everything up again. That made me feel horrible. I was charged with two attempted murders and was facing at the very least a decade behind bars. I was thinking that I would be in prison for my son's entire childhood and teens. He could be a young man before I was released. One of the victims was in hospital for months. I was praying to whatever god might be listening that he would be ok. I didn't want to be responsible for killing him. I didn't want to be charged with murder and spend the next 25 years in prison.

It is hard to describe that feeling. I don't know that I can. During that period of time, to describe my mental state, I think utter despair is as close to the mark as I can get. All the while maintaining a composed exterior, I definitely did not want to appear to be a sook.

Everyone is going through their own shit. Most of us are experiencing the worst time of our lives or at least having a shit time. We are all missing home, kids, partners, having financial trouble, worried, stressed etc. No one wants to hear or see you being a sook about how hard you are doing it. Everyone is going through the same thing and is managing to hold it together, so you can too. That's the expectation. Guys who complain and whinge about their own circumstances get pulled up quite quickly. Often, the attitude is that if you want to whinge and complain, you'll be given something to really whinge and complain about, after which they will likely be told to leave the unit. I'm mainly talking about being on remand here, when inmates first come into prison newly charged with their offence.

To make matters worse for me, my right arm was broken. I had been shot by the guy I had stabbed and was in hospital (yes, I took a knife to a gun fight), the bullet hitting one of the bones in my forearm breaking it. I was in a lot of pain physically, emotionally, mentally, and spiritually. I was in the horrors. At rock bottom.

It was during this time at absolute rock bottom that I made the decision that I had to change my ways. I couldn't go on living this way any longer. Regardless of how long I was going to spend in prison or what I had to do, I would sort my shit out to ensure I never returned to prison again.

Now, that's easy to say, but how was I going to do it? I had no idea. All I knew is that I was determined to find out and see it through.

I asked to participate in some of the courses run at the gaol, addressing drug and alcohol abuse and violent offending/aggression. But I was told I wasn't allowed, as I was not sentenced for my offence yet. I couldn't believe that someone on as serious charges as I, who was willing and had reached a turning point where I wanted to address my issues, would be turned away. To add to my frustration, there were available positions within the course, so I wouldn't be taking up someone else's spot. Despite multiple attempts at pleading my case and pointing out these facts, I was still told no. I then requested to undertake some sort of tertiary education by correspondence; if I was going to serve a very lengthy sentence, I wanted to upskill and better myself with some qualification I could get out with and put to good use. Again, I was denied. I made multiple requests to do the offending addressing courses and tertiary education over an 18-month period but was continually turned away. Over that same time period, I made many requests to speak with the gaol's psychologist. I wanted to work with them and get some advice on how to get to the core of my issues that were causing my offending and other problems in my life, but they were busy dealing with other higher priority cases. I wasn't suicidal, self-harming, or having crazy episodes yelling, screaming, and banging my head against the wall, so I wasn't a priority.

I ended up paying for my own psychologist to come in a few times, but that was mostly for an assessment to provide to the court to explain my mental state at the time of the offence rather than treatment. I also had very little money. I was already broke from paying lawyers to represent me on my previous matters over the last few years, plus not earning a living while incarcerated for that time. I just couldn't afford to have her continue to come in beyond those few assessment sessions. It became apparent to me that I was not going to get any help in here. I would just have to figure it out for myself.

Looking back, all these setbacks were greatly beneficial for me. I had to do the work myself, soul searching hours upon hours. Days, months, and years of reflection figuring it all out. I read anything I could get my hands on. I spoke to people about their own experiences regarding offending, prison, drug and alcohol use, upbringing, and relationships. I was on a mission to understand myself and others, all of which gave me the knowledge to effectively work on my own issues and ultimately the content for my poetry.

One thing I have learnt along the way is that people will only change something once they are ready and decide to. It doesn't matter what that change may be, whether that's quitting smoking, drugs, alcohol, gambling, or criminal offending. It could be a decision to get in shape, eat healthier, be faithful in relationships, or any myriad of changes people might make.

Try convincing a smoker to quit the habit. You could pile evidence to the ceiling about the detrimental health effects of smoking cigarettes. Regardless of the case you make about the financial benefits or the statistics on dying young, they just won't do it until they want to. The government banned advertising, implemented generic packaging, put those awful images of diseased and dying people on the packet, and increased the cost greatly through heavy taxation, but people still smoke.

Until they want to and come to the decision for themselves, they won't make the change, and this is true of all things people change or do not. When someone in custody reaches that point where they want to make positive changes in their lives and there is no help at all to facilitate it, it can really have a detrimental effect on the person. In many circumstances, they will become so frustrated with the situation that they give up on the plan to rehabilitate and continue on with the destructive behaviours that landed them in prison in the first place. Often, they will push back even harder against the system. It is common to hear guys say things like, 'We are set up to fail. The system is against us.' How could you blame anyone for thinking this way in that situation. I experienced this frustration myself, but I was determined to push through it. I remained focused on working on myself regardless of the setbacks. Fuck doing this 'in and out of prison' routine forever.

Let me tell you, there is no help whatsoever anywhere within the prison system, that's for sure. This lack of help for those who want and need it is a major contributing factor to the endless crime and recidivism problem in this country. As discussed earlier in the 'Recidivism' chapter, there is no genuine effort made at all within the prison system to rehabilitate offenders while in custody, not even for those who actively seek out help.

I have learnt a great deal off the back of the setbacks I had at the beginning of this sentence, being deeply depressed, turned away time and time again after seeking help, and forced to work it all out for myself. It was the start of my growth and self-development journey, and like most of these journeys, it spawned out of adversity. Adversity is life's greatest teacher and a source of an incredible amount of growth potential if we choose to view it through that lens. But I have dedicated the next chapter to 'adversity', so I will leave it at that for now.

The experience of returning to prison this time was the lowest point of my life. The hardest phone call of my life was to my son, telling him I was back in prison again after promising him I would never return. The disappointment in his voice was crushing. Being disappointed in yourself is one thing, but letting down those you love, disappointing them, and causing them pain is horrible. I hated myself for a long time for that. Sometimes, it takes a lot of pain before we take corrective action to sort out the shit we have to in our lives. This was the case for me, and I am determined to never put my loved ones or myself in that situation again. It takes determination, effort, and hard work to see it through. Make the choice, apply these principles, and there is nothing that cannot be overcome.

'Success is not final, failure is not fatal; it is the courage to continue that counts.'

—Winston Churchill

'Failure is simply the opportunity to begin again, this time more intelligently.'

—Henry Ford

Coming Back

I cannot get any lower.
I have fallen into the abyss once more.
How have I let this happen?
I feel numb as the guard slams the cell door.

I swore not to return.
I have broken my promise to not come back.
Once again, I have let you down.
My family, I'm sorry; more torture on the rack.

I never mean to hurt you.
I know you suffer when I go away.
This isn't your fault.
My son, I love you; I will miss you every single day.

Never have I felt so bad.
This is rock bottom beyond any other low.
Yet, I just keep digging.
How far into despair can I possibly go?

I thought this was behind me.
Now I'm stuck back at square one.
A new court case,
Years ahead; how badly things have come undone?

But from the ashes,
Just like the phoenix, I will be reborn.
From rock bottom, up
Is the only way out, bouncing back once more.

To turn things around
Will take effort; I am committed to being better.
I will do whatever it takes.
Today I begin, willing to fight with a vendetta.

To change my ways,
Doing the work to ensure I never return.
Addressing my issues won't be easy.
Letting everyone down again would be a thousand times worse.

The road ahead is ugly,
With so many twists and turns.
At the end is treasure,
The prize true freedom that this time I've earned.

Adversity

Out of all the poems I have written, I believe this one has the greatest potential to have a positive impact if the message can be understood. Understanding the role adversity plays in our lives and the power in learning how to effectively use it by viewing it in another light is exponential. Simply reframing the way in which we view the hardships we face – from a purely negative experience to one of learning, growth potential, and opportunity – has the power to immediately take some of the sting out of whatever it is we are going through. This can be the first step towards working through the issue rather than feeling stuck in the middle of it with no way out. That switch from a negative mindset to one of positivity allows us to begin working on the issue in a constructive way. Once you are able to take this constructive approach, you are on the road to overcoming the adversity for which you will be stronger, wiser, and armoured for whatever trouble comes later.

What do I mean when I say adversity? I define adversity as anything difficult in your life, any hardship you endure.

Losing your job, that sucks. That's adversity. A relationship break down and the emotional pain you go through as a result, adversity. Suffering an injury, having a car accident, being scammed, beaten up, robbed, financial hardship, illness, etc., you get the drift. Anything that causes us to suffer in some way. For some, it may not be something that happens to them like being robbed. It can be struggling with mental health issues or a drug addiction. Maybe someone's suffering is related to self-esteem issues or self-doubt. Whatever the cause, hardship comes in many different forms. We all have to go through it one way or another. No one wants to suffer adversity, but it's an absolute certainty that we all do.

The idea of viewing adversity in a positive light, being an opportunity, may seem very odd. I can feel some of you now thinking that it sounds like utter stupidity. 'Who the fuck is going to be happy about being robbed, Scott, you idiot!' Well, no one wants to be robbed. No one wants to suffer any form of adversity at all. Whether we want to or not is beside the point. It's going to happen, again and again, regardless of how we feel about it. You don't have a choice in the matter. The choice you do have, however, is how you deal with that adversity when it inevitably rears its head. When something does go wrong, the initial response is usually, 'What the fuck!' It comes as a shock. We are rarely expecting trouble when it comes, nor are we prepared for it. It usually happens out of the blue when we least expect it. After the initial shock, the next response is, 'Why me,' feeling as though bad luck is unfairly focusing her attention on us. This is a negative victim mentality that doesn't serve us in any constructive way, but it is also a natural response. To be able to recognise it for what it is and then set it aside is a skill worth developing. Now, whether you know it or not, at this point you are faced with a choice: deal with whatever has happened in either a constructive or destructive manner.

Who has had a big argument with their partner, stormed out of the house, and gone out drinking? Fairly common male response. I have done this a hundred times.

Or ladies, have you gone out shopping, blowing the budget on new shoes, a dress, a handbag, hair and nails, and a night out with the girls to vent about how much of a prick he is? Satisfying, yes. Constructive? No.

As good as it may feel at the time to further piss your partner off, scoring a few extra points against them, it is only adding more fuel to the burning issues that lead to the arguing in the first place. It contributes nothing constructive towards solving the problems going on.

A more serious example of choosing to deal with adversity in a destructive manner is using drugs and/or alcohol as a coping mechanism. Substance abuse, self-medicating to get through some current or past hardship or trauma, is both very destructive and very common. I am guilty of dealing with the issues in my life in a destructive way in the past. I think we can all lay claim to it at some point. I have turned to drugs and alcohol to self-medicate, leading to bigger problems, which was a major contributing factor to almost all the trouble I ever found myself in with the law, in relationships, and life in general. That led to me finding myself in prison on multiple occasions. This a very familiar story in prison. Although ending up in prison is an extreme outcome, it's where the road leads for quite a lot of people. People who would never have thought they'd ever find themselves locked up suddenly find themselves inside, asking, 'How did I end up in here?' When someone finds themselves drinking alcohol or using drugs, either illicit or prescription, to self-medicate, it rarely ends well. Mostly, the consequences of that would be health related, both physical and mental. However, it can go beyond that, often causing relationship problems, employment problems, and financial hardship, and sometimes legal consequences.

So how can adversity be beneficial?

Let me frame it this way. When life is all smooth sailing, who stops and takes stock of why things are going so well? No one. We are too busy basking in god's good favour, enjoying the good things in life that we no doubt deserve. We think this is how it should be. Or at the very least, we are cruising along oblivious to anything going on that is not negatively affecting us.

It's when things aren't going so well that eventually we ask why. This is the beginning of personal growth and development. This is the beginning of learning.

Let's say the hardship is being fired from your job. Why were you fired? Did you call in sick on Monday too often? Were you lazy? Could you have been more productive rather than ducking out for a dozen cigarette breaks? Could you have made more of an effort to improve on the areas that were not your strong points?

If you don't want to be fired in the future, you might take a constructive view of the situation. You could accept that you made those mistakes; commit to cutting back on the big weekends that were causing you to be wrecked on Mondays; either reduce or eliminate the smoke breaks, using the experience to motivate you to cut back on or quit the cigarettes; make a conscious effort to be more productive at the next job; along with improving on those skills that need some developing. That is an example of taking a shitty situation, flipping on its head, and having a beneficial effect. That is choosing to view adversity through a new lens and having it work for you rather than against you. It is a choice.

The alternative is to play the victim, taking the destructive approach. You could tell your boss to go and fuck themselves (I done exactly that on one occasion), take the view that you have been unfairly targeted (after all, other employees go for smoke breaks, other employees take days off, etc.), and take the same poor attitude into the next job.

Setting the ego aside, facing up to our mistakes, and holding ourselves accountable isn't always easy. But if you let your ego make the decisions, it will almost always take the destructive path. Making the choice to deal with adversity in a constructive way, viewing it as a learning experience, is usually going to be the hard option. At least at first. Like anything worth doing, it will likely be hard at first, but with practice and understanding, it gets easier and easier until it becomes habit.

In 2018, I came back to prison for the third time. This is when I finally asked myself why. 'How the fuck have I ended up back here again?' is closer to how I would've phrased it. I couldn't believe it. But once I took stock of the situation, assessing what I had been doing that had led up to the offence and subsequent arrest, it was no surprise at all I was back again. It was in that deep, dark hole that I had dug for myself that I gazed inwards long and hard and just broke down. I hit rock bottom so hard, at speed, head first. Splat! I felt psychologically, emotionally, and spiritually broken. I had let down everyone who had supported me through the previous two occasions I found myself incarcerated and through some very hard times for both them and myself. I had broken my promise not to return to prison only eight weeks after my previous release. To say I felt like scum would be seriously understating it. It was the first time in my life that I can honestly say I felt completely selfless in my life. I didn't care about myself or my situation. I didn't feel sorry for myself at all. My only thoughts were for the people I had let down and hurt. Although I didn't realise it at the time, this was a complete dissolving of my ego. If only it had lasted, as it rarely does.

Trying to find some positive in the situation at that time was definitely like trying to find a needle in a hay stack. I hadn't even begun working on myself at that point. I hadn't developed any of the philosophies or tools around self-development I write about in this book. This was day one of my learning journey. I had no idea how to make the changes I needed to make. I had no answers. All I could muster in that moment was to commit to finding out. I was determined to learn how to resolve the issues that were causing me to repeatedly fuck everything up so badly. Never again, I vowed. I couldn't allow this to continue to happen.

As much as all this time in prison has been shit, and believe me when I say it has been very shit, there has been such a wealth of growth and self-development I have been able to squeeze out of it, once I decided to reframe the view I took.

At the beginning of this chapter, when I mentioned growth potential and opportunity, I followed the word growth with potential. Any adversity, each shit situation you find yourself facing, has the potential of being beneficial, providing the opportunity for personal growth, should you seize that opportunity. That's up to you. It's a decision. It is a decision I had to make, and once I did, I was able to begin the process of picking myself up from the cold, hard floor of rock bottom. I was able to start working out how I could constructively address the issues that had been ruining my life. This was all a long process. I didn't have any answers for some time, but at least I was asking the right questions of myself now. I was making a genuine effort to walk along this new path towards bettering myself.

Life has a way of teaching us the lessons we need to learn at that time, and it can be a harsh teacher. Life will punish us with the consequences, and it's up to us to figure out why. If we fail to work it out, it will continue dishing out more punishment.

This is the equivalent of your dad coming home when you're a kid, taking off his belt, and smacking you with it. No warning, no explanation. Your young kid mind would be shocked, thinking, 'What was that for?' Dad comes in again five minutes later and whack! Another lash with the belt. You'd ask this time, 'What was that for?' He'd respond, 'Figure it out,' leaving you to think it over.

Well, that's how life teaches us as well. Often, there are plenty of warning signs that we need to make a course adjustment. For those tuned in enough to read the signs and make the necessary corrections, they can avoid the punishment. I was not one of these people. I was continually making the same mistakes over and over. The signs were there; I just failed to notice them. So life continued to punish me.

Constructively working on the issues in your life takes honesty with yourself. If you cannot be honest with yourself, you are wasting your time. It is not easy looking in the mirror and holding yourself to account for your failings. However, to grow and overcome your shortfalls, it is absolutely necessary.

Most of what I have discussed around adversity to this point has focused on mistakes and shortfalls that we are at fault for. A great deal of the adversity we face will in some way be brought on by our own actions, but not always. I will go back to something I mentioned at the beginning of the chapter about being scammed, beaten up, or robbed. These types of things happen to us rather than happening because of us. It is still adversity, just no blame can be attributed to us for it, which for some makes it a bitter pill to swallow. How can these things be beneficial? Well, the answer is that none of these things in and of themself are beneficial. Trust me when I say, getting punched in the face is not beneficial. Crashing your car into a pole, also not great. The adverse event itself may be nothing but bad news; it's what you can potentially gain as a result of it that is good, if you so choose.

Let's use the car accident as the example, an accident for which you are not at fault. Does it matter? The result is the same. The car is still a wreck, and any injuries you sustain hurt just the same regardless of who's at fault. Again, it would be easy to view the situation with a victim mentality. 'Why me?' 'I'm a good person. I'm a good driver. I'm now suffering through no fault of my own. This isn't fair.' Those things may all be true, but what does it matter?

You can think this way all you like. It will not change the current situation you are in, nor can you learn or grow from the experience. You are actually likely to suffer more, feeling sorry for yourself and becoming depressed and miserable.

So how exactly can we take something positive out of this scenario?

You may reflect on the car accident and contemplate your own mortality; you very well could have died, after all. With that perspective, certain things you had been worrying about may now seem insignificant. You may prioritise family time over a busy social schedule with people who now all of a sudden don't seem as important to you. You could visit your parents more often and tell your kids and partner you love them each day before leaving the house. Take that holiday you have been talking about for years, finish that book you started writing long ago, or just appreciate the simple things a little more.

At the time, the event seems nothing but horrible, but in time, after taking some positives from it that end up improving your life, you may just look back at it as a blessing in disguise. I have heard just that from many people who have suffered some kind of hardship as a result of something unexpected happening to them, some actually having been injured in car accidents. A relative of mine lost his leg in a car crash and looks back at the event that almost killed him as the thing that probably saved his life. He used the hardship as a turning point and made changes to better himself. He is now in training for the Paralympic Winter Games.

It's up to you how you view any situation. If you can learn to deal with adversity in a constructive way, you will be able to gain something positive from it. Of this, I am certain.

Whatever form of adversity we face, it offers us the opportunity to build strength, resilience, and personal growth. Just enduring hardship, regardless of how we deal with it, makes us stronger. Recognising the strength it took just to get through a tough situation in itself is viewing it through a positive lens. If that is all the positivity you can manage to squeeze from it, then it is still constructive. You will be able to take that new strength and confidence into the next tough situation. It will thicken your armour, helping to absorb some of the blow.

Enduring any hardship is not fun. We want nothing but smooth sailing for our voyage through life, but that's not how it goes. Rough seas are par for the course. Sunny days and smooth sailing are nice and always welcome, but the weather will always turn at some point, and like any good sailor, we must too be prepared to deal with it when it does.

Changing the way we view these turns of fortune that we all inevitably face, learning to take the positives from the experience, and building up resilience is how we prepare for the next bought of adversity. This in itself is one of the lessons life wants us to learn. She will keep sending trouble our way, whether we learn to deal with it or not. Like all things that are difficult that we prepare for, we just get better with practice. I have described adversity as life's weight set in a previous chapter. Just like any athlete who trains their body, placing it under strain is how the body becomes conditioned and strong. Adversity and hardship condition your mind and will power in the same way. It is under extreme heat and constant hammering that the strongest steel is forged. Diamonds form under extreme heat and pressure. Take this view of adversity, and forge the strongest version of yourself imaginable. Learn to seek out the utility in hardship. Not only will you be heavily armoured to deal with whatever comes next, you will sail head first into life with a new confidence to go anywhere you so choose.

'Hard times create strong men; strong men create good times;

Good times create weak men; weak men create hard times.'

—unknown

'No man is more unhappy than he who never faces adversity. For he is not permitted to prove himself.'

—Seneca

Adversity

When times are good,
All seems to have fallen in place,
We don't gaze inward.
There is no need to assess time and space.

It is easy to falsely believe
That calm seas will prevail the trip.
This is usually when
Fierce winds pick up causing our sails to rip.

Adversity we must suffer.
It is through pain that we grow tough.
None can avoid it,
For life teaches us her lessons thus.

We all must endure
Our own trials, battles, and tribulations.
Emerging the other side
With thicker armour and extra insulation.

Adversity hardens the will,
The way the hammer and fire temper steel.
There is no greater method
To prepare for life's next ride downhill.

So tackle troubles head on,
Embracing the process to come.
This golden life opportunity,
Gain wisdom, grow strong beating your battle drum.

Missing Home

One of the aims of this book is let the reader into the mind of someone in prison. I want to convey the experience, thoughts, and feelings we have while we are in here. I hope I can do that well enough to allow you to feel as though you now know what it's like walking in these shoes.

This poem expresses the typical thoughts that often go through the mind of a prisoner when we are lying in bed at night in our cell missing home. Anyone who finds themselves in prison has regrets. I'm yet to meet someone who is happy to be here and wouldn't change a thing given the opportunity. We all wish we could go back and do things differently when we find ourselves in a shit situation. It's very common to find yourself stuck thinking of all the things you are missing out on, wishing we hadn't fucked things up so badly. Stressing about money, what's going on outside, the court case, will I get bail, the kids, etc., this is referred to as doing head miles. Head miles are not fun, but it is easy to get stuck thinking about these things over and over. Regularly. This is especially so while on remand and everything is uncertain and new. Your world is in a spin, and you're just trying to get your bearings and get a handle on the situation.

It wouldn't come as any surprise that while we are in prison, we miss home a lot. I also assume that no one is under any illusion about the prison being an uncomfortable place in every sense of the word. I miss many things, and somewhere very near the top of that list is my comfortable bed. Fuck, I miss my bed. As you can surely imagine, the beds in gaol are rubbish. They are so shit. A thin piece of foam wrapped in protective plastic on a metal frame, along with a foam pillow wrapped in the same plastic. Everyone in here complains about having a sore lower back. Neck and shoulder issues are also very common. Chiropractors and physiotherapists rub their hands together when someone walks into their practice after having spent time in prison.

It is like a crashed car being towed into the panel beaters shop; it is going to take some serious work to straighten everything out. Well, that is how my spine feels after seven years of sleeping on gaol mattresses. Trust me when I say that when spending time in prison, you miss your bed.

Above everything else, I miss my son the most. I am very aware that I can never get back this time. There is no way to ever make up that time, missing out on a big portion of his childhood. It is the biggest regret and failure of my life. Anyone in prison with children would agree that missing their kids and not being around for them is the hardest part of being incarcerated. We miss the simple things, like giving them a hug, picking them up from school, weekend sports, and tucking them into bed. It's these simple little things that we take for granted that hurt the most when we lose them. It is strong motivation to make positive changes and get things back on track once released. For some, that's easier than for others, but for the guys with kids, having that as a motivating factor helps.

One of the most common things I hear guys say that they want to do once released is that they can't wait to go to the beach and dive into the water. I guess when people think of freedom, the beach is one of those images that comes to mind. Diving in and swimming under the waves is such a good feeling that it seems to be what freedom feels like to someone who has had it taken away from them. I remember the first time I came in, it was one of the things I looked forward to doing the most. Until you find yourself in a situation in which you are without something important to you, something that you take having for granted, it can be hard to really appreciate the things you are lucky to have. Being in prison, just like any other adversity, afforded me the opportunity to gain new perspective on many things.

Obviously, freedom is one of those things. Being free to jump in the car, head down to the beach and dive under the waves, feeling the fresh salt water washing over my skin is such a luxury that I look forward to being able to enjoy again. It was something I never appreciated up until the point when it wasn't an option.

Another obvious luxury we all have to adjust to being without and miss while we are in custody is sex. No women, no sex. Prison is not what most people imagine. No one is being raped. Sex offenders of any kind are despised among the prison population. Homosexual sex is almost non-existent. There are obviously gay men in prison, and I have heard of the odd instance when inmates have sex, but it's very rare. So 99.9% go without sex while in prison. Apparently, the women's prisons are different. From what I hear, the saying in the women's prison system is 'gay for the stay'. Going without sex for years on end is no fun at all. We all miss the touch of a women. Just conversing with women and enjoying their company is something that is noticeably absent. The conversations between men are very different than between men and women. Taking romance/sex out of the equation, just missing that balance that speaking with women offers is missed. I've had conversations with guys in here about losing touch talking to women. It is likely going to be a bit messy trying to get that confidence back once released. I see a fair bit of rejection in my future until I get back into the swing of things. Talking with women is all about confidence; a lack of confidence in a man is very apparent to women. Females pick up on this like a shark smells blood in the water. This is something we lose touch with after serving long gaol terms, so please go easy on me, ladies.

When I'm laying down at night missing home, my son, my family, friends, women, my freedom in general, it is always followed by regret. I am constantly aware of what a waste of time and life this all is.

I know I can't change what's has happened in the past. I can't ever go back to undo my mistakes, no matter how much I wish I could. I am stuck in this situation and must deal with the consequences. The only value in looking back is to do our best to learn from the mistakes of the past in order to do better in the future. I definitely don't want to be in this position again, missing home, causing those close to me to suffer. These thoughts repeat again and again at night when I'm lying in my cell.

One of many important things I will take away from this experience is not taking for granted all the things I'm currently missing. I will make every effort to show appreciation to those in my life who deserve it. I think one of the best ways to do that other than vocalising and expressing it to them is to be stable, reliable, and successful, getting back to enjoying a normal life free from all the trouble, leaving it all behind me as I walk out of the prison gates.

> *'It's a funny thing coming home. Nothing changes. Everything looks the same, feels the same, even smells the same. You realise what's changed is you.'*
>
> —F Scott Fitzgerald

Missing Home

Some nights, I lay awake,
Travelling a thousand miles in my head.
But the only place
I want to go is home to my own bed.

I miss my son each day.
I long to just hang out with my boy.
Kick a football with him,
Play PlayStation, buy him a new toy.

How good it will be,
To spend the day at Bondi beach.
Go for a drive,
Attend the footy, jet ski at Freemans Reach.

How long will it be,
Before I can feel a women's touch?
Going out, picking up,
God, I miss those times so much.

I can't wait to see my family
And spend time with all my friends.
What a waste of life it is here.
How long until this nightmare ends?

So much I am missing out on.
This time I can't ever gain back.
Once I'm finally out of here,
This time I'll get my life back on track.

Karma

Every action has a reaction; cause and effect. This is the very basic principle of karma. We have all heard the old adages 'What goes around comes around' and 'You reap what you sow.' This concept of karma seems intrinsically imbedded in our psyche. Why is that?

Perhaps it has something to do with our association with being punished for being naughty and rewarded for good behaviour as children. The laws and the consequences of breaking them governing society too. Maybe, but I think it is much more than that. I have seen far too much of the phenomenon of karma in action for it to be simply categorised as this.

If we think and act in a positive manner (the cause), we should enjoy positive results (the effect). If you punch someone in the face (action), they'll likely punch you back, and you may find yourself in trouble with the law (reaction). Nowhere is suffering the consequences of negative actions more evident than finding yourself in prison. Not only are you suffering your own punishment, but you are also seeing firsthand the harm caused to others. Drug cooks and dealers mix with the very people who ruin themselves using their product. As I've mentioned multiple times in previous chapters, prison is a violent environment. The guy dishing out the violence one day is the victim the next. People from rival groups and families run into one another. Often, each side is in prison for perpetrating violence against the other. In some segregation units, rivals who have killed each other's family members are housed only a few cells apart, yelling out the most horrible shit imaginable about the others loved one's death. Each has caused the other and their family terrible pain. Who wins in that scenario? Their actions caused that karma.

If you watch the news on television, read it in the newspaper, online news feed, etc., however you free folk get your news now, you'll know that crime reporting features heavily. It is full of drug busts, police raids, gang wars, shootings, stabbings, murders, police pursuits, fraud cases, robberies, and plenty more. After the news day is done, the newspapers are thrown out, and the digital feeds fill up with new content. Those offenders featured in yesterday's stories all end up here. I've spent long enough in here to have seen them all and spent plenty of time with every kind. Big names to nobodys, for every type of offence. Many of the big names are dead now or serving lengthy prison terms. They carve a path to the top of the criminal world through violence, fear, and intimidation. They make big money for a while, and with that comes a big target on their back, from both rivals and the police. Forever.

Enemies accumulate, and eventually, someone else comes up and takes over, eliminating the guy/guys at the top. And on and on it goes. The perpetrators of the violence become the victims of it.

Karma. If you create the cause, you will suffer the effects. I've seen drug dealers and cooks become hooked on the same product they produced and supplied. They ruin themselves the same way they have their customers. I'm mainly referring to the drug ice, but it is also true of heroin and to a lesser extent cocaine. Ice is the worst one of all. It's an insidious drug that I've stayed right away from. I've watched it destroy people time and time again. Almost anyone who uses it regularly ends up fucked. We call it 'cooked or fried'. It's as though they have fried their brains circuitry in much the same way as a PC board can be fried. They suffer serious and often permanent mental health issues, which is quite common. They destroy themselves using this drug. My advice is to stay right away from it.

There are obviously bullies in prison. They stand over (intimidate) people, taking their food and belongings off them and even getting them to have their families deposit money into outside bank accounts to avoid being assaulted; often, just because they can, intimidating people out of boredom but usually to support a drug habit. They often get away with it, but eventually, they always cop it in the end. They pick the wrong person, some unassuming, innocent-looking guy who just happens to be able to look after themselves. I've seen this happen more times than I can count. Everyone loves seeing a bully cop it. They get their karma too.

Whether in prison or out in society, you never really know who you're dealing with, unless of course that person is known to you. You may be arguing with a psychopath, a black belt in jiu jitsu, a special forces operator, or an up-and-coming boxer. Some of the most dangerous and capable guys I know are completely unassuming. Usually, the steroid abusing, heavily tattooed guys can't fight for shit. It's the guys who look anything but dangerous who are the ones to really worry about. I have seen a lot of men come undone both in prison and outside these walls by making the mistake of underestimating someone and suffering a rude shock.

Treat people well, regardless of who they are or what your perception of them is, and they will likely treat you the same way in return. Do good things, and good things will happen to you. Think positively, and positive things will come into your life. Do the opposite, and you'll just as likely get the opposite in return. This is how karma works. It's that simple. Common sense really, when you take a second to think about it.

And sure, bad things do happen to good people, while good things also happen to terrible people. Both good and bad fortune befalls us all. That's just life. None of us get through life unscathed, no matter how good a person we are.

Adversity, which we've already covered, occurs to teach the lessons we need to learn, allowing us to grow. Through this process, we become better human beings. With karma, sometimes a person just gets exactly what they deserve. That's their lesson and an opportunity for them to learn and grow to become a better person.

In the sixth paragraph of this poem, I had someone specific in mind who had caused a great deal of heartache and misery to a lot of people. He was a callous and ruthless man, karma dealing with him accordingly. Those type of people never last long.

Sir Isaac Newton, a famed 17th- and 18th-century physicist, best known for his universal theory of gravity in one of the most famous physics papers ever written, often referred to simply as the *Principia*, also famously formulated the laws of motion, of which there are three laws. The third law states that for every action (force) in nature, there is an equal and opposite reaction. Applied to the current topic of karma, the law seems very appropriate. I've tweaked the wording slightly in the poem from opposite reaction to proportionate reaction, which to me at least sums up the phenomenon of karma perfectly. We receive our karma both good and bad in direct proportion to our causal thoughts and actions. Sir Isaac Newton's findings in the physical world also seem relevant in the conceptual sense, perhaps a universal law that exists across all planes.

To go back to the scenario of you punching someone in the face, to receive a punch back and possibly be charged with assault is proportionate. To be assaulted at some later date finding out how it feels to be on the receiving end is proportionate. To be hit by a truck losing both arms and both legs is not. In my experience and observation, karma is proportionate.

In the section 'The Time Is Now', I discuss finding happiness in what is good in our lives right now. One way to cultivate a little more happiness is through altruistic action. Simply doing something kind for someone else, acting charitably for the benefit of others, is not only good for those benefitting from your actions. It makes you feel good within yourself as well. It is a nice little dose of instant karma that is mutually beneficial. To have compassion for other people, understanding that others are suffering their own problems and adversity, rather than just being focused on what's going on with you, has great power in taking some of the focus off your own problems, often providing some perspective or at least just taking your mind of it all for a while. Acting charitably has healing power in and of itself. Your intention to be of benefit to someone else has the unintended effect of being beneficial for yourself. It is a win-win scenario. Imagine the difference it would make if we all adopted just a small amount of this way of thinking. Positive thinking plants the seeds for positive action; positive action reaps positive rewards.

That is karma in a nutshell.

> *'Our life is shaped by our mind, for we become what we think.'*
>
> —Buddha

Karma

Do unto others,
As you would have others do to you.
An old proverb
To consider in all that we do.

What goes around comes around,
Another that never fails to ring true.
Also known as karma,
What we give to the world will come back to you.

Whether good or evil,
We all reap the seeds we sow.
What do you have growing?
The answer only you yourself know.

Time and time again,
I've seen this phenomenon in action.
This law of cause and effect,
Every action having an equal and proportionate reaction.

I've witnessed the bully
Become the victim too many times to count.
And watched the fraudster
Pay a price greater than the stolen amount.

The worst of humanity,
Who ruin families' lives without remorse,
This ruthless, murdering gangster
Dies alone a junkie; his callous life's run its course.

I am not all that religious,
But there is truth in the concept of karma.
Regardless of your faith,
Enjoy this wisdom from the Dalai Lama.

Have compassion for one another.
We are all human beings who don't want to suffer.
If you seek happiness,
Act in a way that brings happiness to others.

Day In, Day Out

There is nothing fun or exciting about day-to-day life in prison. It is groundhog day over and over again. Generally, nothing good happens. Mind numbing boredom is how I would sum up day-to-day life in here.

Depending on your circumstances and where you are in the legal process, I would add stress and frustration into the mix. I felt a lot of frustration at not being able to access the help I was seeking, which I have already discussed. I felt frustration at not being able to make any progress with the academic courses I wanted to access, my general life situation and wanting to get out to pursue the goals I set for myself, and wanting to work on building my relationship with my son. If you want to know what it feels like being in prison, understanding how it feels to experience frustration, boredom, and stress for an extended period of time will give you a fairly good insight.

To combat these emotions, a lot of guys turn to drugs; in fact, most do. Drug use is rampant in the gaol system, which adds to the volatility. People are either as high as kite or hanging out doing whatever it takes to get the drugs they need to feed their addiction. Some of us use exercise as an escape. It is a constructive way to kill time, as well as being great for our mental health. It is the perfect way to combat the very stress, frustration, and boredom everyone is desperately trying to get away from with drugs. Physical training is a big part of the gaol culture, which I have found vital to getting through my time in here. It also pays to be fit and strong to portray strength. It sends a message that if someone tries to fuck with you, they should expect a fit and hard opponent. If you spend time in prison, it is likely you're going to have to fight at some point. That strength and conditioning will come in very handy.

Most gaols offer employment in the laundry, kitchen, or as a wing sweeper, which entails handing out meals and cleaning. None of these jobs pay much at all. The pay is terrible, usually $20–30 a week. Working is just another way to kill the boredom and get out of the pod/yard. In some prisons, there are designated working units that are generally more relaxed and cleaner with slightly better conditions. For many, this is incentive enough to work. I've spent time in working units along with a lot of time in the non-working units. From my experience, the working units a far better. Just the fact that they are much cleaner and more relaxed without near as much trouble was enough for me. After years in hectic yards with plenty of drama, violence, and tension. I'd take clean and quiet any day. Others would say that the working units are boring, as there aren't as much drugs available in them, which is a major deterrent for those who want to get high every day. This happens to be a part of the major appeal to the non-drug users who would rather exercise instead.

Different correctional centres have different routines. At some centres, inmates are locked out in the yard all day. In others, some have access to the unit to shower or cook food before being locked into the cells. While in prison, we spend a large majority of our time locked in cell, on average 18+ hours per day in the maximum security system. Lock-in days are very common in the maximum security prisons due to understaffing and regular incidents. On these days, we stay locked in our cell all day. Depending on which centre you are housed at, as many as three or four lock-in days per week wouldn't be uncommon. Longbay Prison is particularly renowned for these lock-in days. It was the worst place I have been for lock-ins, and I have been to a fair amount of the state's prisons. You are either bored in the yard or bored in your cell most of the time. Just because you are bored doesn't necessarily mean nothing is happening. As stated in the poem, the place is a fucking circus. At any time, things can kick off. Fights occur regularly, and the squad (the incident response officers) will come running in when an incident occurs, often indiscriminately spraying OC spray (capsicum/pepper spray) on anyone in the vicinity. They will usually make everyone get on the ground and lock the entire unit into their cells for the rest of the day.

There are many factors that contribute to the volatility of prison. People are dealing with major legal issues, being separated from loved ones, financial stress, relationship breakdowns, the guards being arseholes, and mental health issues which are extremely prevalent in the prison system. So many other variables contribute to the stress everyone is experiencing, but you get the drift. These are factors that on their own are tough for anyone to deal with at the best of times, let alone dealing with multiples of these issues together from the worst environment imaginable.

Surely, it is easy to see why things kick off in here, often triggered over the most trivial of reasons. Fights over the phone line or a game of cards are common. Confrontations with guards occur from time to time. The guards are often rude to us, and someone who is having a particularly bad day and is at the end of their tether can just snap. When a guard is assaulted, we all cop it. The person or people who attack a guard will really cop it: a severe beating, months of segregation, and further criminal charges for assault. We will all at the very least be locked in cell for multiple days, despite having nothing to do with the incident. Sometimes, someone just starts trouble because they are bored and it's something to do. I was in segregation with a guy who would fight the guards regularly because he was bored. He had been in segregation for years for killing his cell mate. After being in segregation for so long and being bored out of his mind, he would surprise attack a guard who opened his door. When I asked him why he had attacked the guard, he would say, 'Something to do.' Maybe they had been rude to him months earlier, and he hadn't forgotten about it. I have also seen this happen in the yard: someone attacking another inmate or guard because they want to move to another prison or go to segregation.

This is why it pays to be fit and be able to look after yourself; sometimes, someone is targeted for no apparent reason. You're less likely to be considered a target if you appear to be a tough opponent. Even so, this doesn't guarantee you won't be.

I was picked by a guy on my first day at Lithgow Prison. I had just arrived, having been transferred from another gaol. I was assigned a cell along with the other occupant of it. Most cells hold two inmates at a time. It is very rare to have a cell to yourself, especially when first arriving at a prison. Single cells are highly sought after, and in any unit, there are usually only a few, if any. I didn't have a choice who I was placed with, as it was the only cell in the unit with a spare bed. The gaol was full at the time, as is common in our overflowing prison system. My new cell mate was adamant that he didn't want anyone in with him. He had immediately kicked out of the cell the last four or five guys who had been unfortunate enough to be placed in with him. He told me as much himself. He said that he had either threatened them or beaten them up to make them leave.

This guy was a big man, standing at 6'2" or 6'3" and about 160 kg. He was a bully and just a real piece of shit. He threw his weight around and treated everyone poorly. He told me that he had 'sent' the others that had been placed in with him, and he would send me too. 'Sending' someone means to kick them out of the general population units to the protection units (or boneyard, as we call it). The boneyard is where sex offenders and police informants (dogs) are housed. People who bail or are sent from the main because they are in danger or fear for their safety often choose to go there. Once someone ends up in protection, they become a target of the entire main population to be attacked at any opportunity. For this guy to say he would 'send me' was a massive deal. If someone says they are going to send you and you don't do something about it, the whole yard will turn on you. I had no option but to fight him.

I beat the crap out of this big bully and made sure I'd done a good job of it too. He came out of it battered, bloody, and bruised. Beaten to a pulp.

I was new to the prison. I didn't know anyone in the unit. I was on my own. He had friends there, but nobody seemed too keen to back him up. It was important to send the message that I was no pushover, and if anyone fucked with me, they could expect a tough fight.

I felt the tension for a few weeks afterwards and heard some whispers in the days after that there might have been some attempt to get me back, but nothing eventuated. I was fairly confident after those initial few weeks that he and his group weren't going to do anything. I had friends in the neighbouring yard who were encouraging me to come over to their unit, but I didn't want to appear to be moving yards to avoid them. Despite hating where I was, I stayed in that shit unit for four months until the bully went home, then I moved. People's perception in prison matters. If you're viewed as weak, it could cause you problems later on, which I was obviously keen to avoid in this circumstance.

Violence is commonplace in here. After a while, you become desensitised to it. Even the most shocking acts to the average person are just seen as another day in here. All sorts of weapons are fashioned in prison out of just about anything you can imagine. 'Slashers' are particularly nasty, made from razor blades melted into a plastic handle. They open up flesh with deep gashes that bleed profusely. I've seen people's faces opened with them many times over, others stabbed with shanks to the head, neck, and face. Often, people are jumped by several guys at a time and are then kicked in the head and even have their heads jumped up and down on while unconscious. It's not always the inmates dishing out the violence. Sometimes, it's the guards beating guys up, breaking wrists and arms of the guys they are restraining. Boiling hot water with jam heated up in a microwave is another nasty weapon that causes deep burns. And plenty, plenty more. Know that if you come to prison, you will be exposed to violence. Mostly, it's just fighting, but occasionally, things can get very serious.

Every year, people are killed in the prison system, and many more suffer severe injuries. Stabbings especially are common place.

I will add that once you progress into the minimum security system, things change a lot. Fights still occur, but the level of violence and stress reduces. Things are generally much more relaxed.

It's up to the individual how they want to do their time. Inmates who want to keep their heads down and avoid issues generally can. Staying away from drugs and working within the gaol is a good start. Most trouble arises from drug debts or tobacco debts. As I've emphasised throughout the book, exercising is another good way to avoid trouble and become friends with other like-minded guys. If you can stay away from the drugs and smoking, keep busy working and training, then you are much less likely to have problems.

Not everyone who finds themselves in prison are terrible people. Most are just normal people who have either made some poor choices or have some issues they need to work on. A small percentage are what you would call career criminals and violent, dangerous men. For the majority who have made poor choices or have some issues to work on, there is not a lot of help to get them on the right track. Nothing about the prison system is conducive to rehabilitation. There is not much to assist self-growth and personal development either. You don't gain skills to take out into society to help you reintegrate and find meaningful employment. In fact, it is quite the opposite. Those with various issues just get worse. Drug dependency and mental health issues decline further.

People without a drug issue coming in develop a habit and leave with one. Non-violent offenders become violent through necessity or influence. Young guys who come into custody for minor offences spend extended periods of time on remand with hardened criminals who influence and recruit them. People develop contacts in the drug game and with gangs. Normal young guys are exposed to violence and receive an apprenticeship in crime. They often return to society fucked up and either drug dependent or with a higher level of criminality with new criminal contacts, and the cycle of recidivism begins for them.

Regardless of your view about how the justice system deals with criminal offending or how the corrective system ought to function, whether that's purely punitive, rehabilitative, or a combination of both, the fact of the matter is that currently, it is almost purely punitive, and it does not work. There is no rehabilitation to be found here. Offenders of all kinds come to prison and mostly just get worse, often returning to prison multiple times for either the same type or more serious offences. Most repeat criminal offending follows an escalating pattern. It is not good for society to have people in custody who are being released time and time again worse than when they entered the system. I can say that this is in large part due to the inefficiencies within the corrective system and complete lack of any effort at all to effectively address issues for guys who are often seeking out help to do so.

Day-to-day prison life is a lot of time ticking by with nothing good or constructive to do. How much better could all this time be spent to ensure people are given every opportunity to rehabilitate? Isn't that what society as a whole would expect to occur? And at the earliest interaction with the system?

Bored people will find ways to fill in their time, and without many options and an abundance of drugs available, that is often the way the time is filled. Guys get up to mischief, start trouble, and keep busy networking and planning how to make some money once they get out.

The place is stressful, dirty, boring, and in every sense of the word shit. It really is a waste of life with nothing good to be gained, and unless someone decides to take the initiative and work hard on sorting out their issues on their own, they are unlikely to change. It is not an easy task, but it is doable. Like always, it's a choice for the individual to make. It's the choice I had to make, and despite all the setbacks, I managed to better myself, as can anyone else who finds themselves in tough circumstances. Yourself included.

'You can have success or excuses; but you can't have both.'

—Scott TK Keighran

Day In, Day Out

The cell door cracks open
To start another day just like the last.
The same old shit,
On the merry-go-round going nowhere fast.

What will today bring?
I'm sure it won't be anything good.
Counting down the days,
If I could take back my mistakes, I would.

Out into the yard
For another day on the frontline,
What battle today holds?
Something physical or combat within the mind.

This can't be rehabilitation,
To it all I have become desensitized.
Here we go again,
It's time to fight the enemy in my eyes.

Boredom fills the days.
I'm trying to find some meaning or purpose.
As I look around me,
I realise I'm stuck in a fucking circus.

There is no help here.
If my life is to change, it's up to me.
I will do the work myself,
To ensure I can truly be set free.

To be free of prison,
In the physical, mental, and metaphorical sense.
I've had enough of this now.
It's no life living behind a barbed wire fence.

To break this cycle,
I will do all in my power.
To make the changes,
Ensuring I don't return, not even for a single hour.

To those I love,
I promise I'm coming home to you.
For good, this time;
I'm a better man; your faith can be renewed.

Your Poem

This the first poem I wrote. Until the moment I picked up a pen and began writing it, I hadn't intended to write a poem. As I mentioned in the preface, it just happened unexpectedly.

In prison, there is obviously a great deal of time to think. We spend a lot of time locked in our cells. Depending on the security classification you're designated and the correctional centre you're housed at, inmates can spend over 18 hours of each day locked in cell; that is, if the normal routine is adhered to. Full day lock-ins, late let-goes, and early lock-ins are very common. We often don't get out due to staff shortages or incidents in the centre. Whatever the reason, we are locked in a lot.

I have spent a great deal of my time in prison contemplating every topic imaginable. I'm interested in cosmology and the mysteries of space, life on earth and how it all began, the true nature of reality. When else in my life would I have more spare time than I do now to just ponder? I am a deep thinker; I always have been. I remember as a young child contemplating the vastness of space and being completely perplexed at the concept of infinite space. Along with these big concepts, I've mostly spent my thinking time while incarcerated focused on things to improve myself, looking at the past analytically and recognising my mistakes to learn, attempting to understand the factors that led me to this place, my experiences both past and present in here to grow, and my plans for the future, my family, and friends.

On this particular occasion, however, I was thinking about a girl. I met this girl on the gold coast while I was out for the night in my mid-20s. She was 19 when we met and one of the prettiest girls I have ever met. We clicked immediately. She lived locally, and I lived in Sydney, but I would travel regularly between home and the gold coast. Long story short, life took us in different directions. We met other people, and a few years later, I ended up in prison. We stayed in contact over the years on and off. We each said that although we met other people, we always thought somehow we would end up together. We have always had a strong connection and attraction to one another.

We have mutual friends, so I get to hear what's going on with her through them, and vis versa. So on this particular evening, I was laying in my cell thinking about her. Without intending to, I started organising my thoughts into verses in the form of a poem. I picked up a pen and wrote it all down. Twenty minutes later, I had written the poem. That was the beginning of my writing of poetry. Once I started writing, they just kept coming one after the other. Like this poem, all the poetry I have written flowed simply from all the thoughts that had been floating around in my head for some time.

As I mentioned I am a deep thinker, so there was quite a bit to get out. Until this point, I had never written or read poetry. I have no idea why my subconscious mind chose poetry as an outlet. It just happened. Most of the topics I write about just flow naturally, because I have spent years contemplating the subject. Some poems take more work than others, but largely, they come without a lot of effort. They seem to write themselves, as was the case with this one.

With the written section of each chapter, these are simply my thoughts, philosophies, and conclusions I have reached behind each poem. I base my opinions off the back of this through my own experience and what I know to be true for myself. I believe in what I have produced wholeheartedly; otherwise, I wouldn't put it out. I stand behind every word. It is honest and authentic, and it's my own experience and the knowledge I have gained from it all. It is my overarching aim in publishing this book that what I have learnt along the way can be of some benefit to whoever reads it. Each poem is a reflection of my thoughts, feelings, and experiences from within these prison walls. Another aim is to convey how it feels to be here, experiencing walking in these shoes. I hope I have done enough to get that across.

This poem is a reminder for me that no matter my life situation, I never know what may be just around the corner. Seemingly out of nowhere, my poetry writing gave me an outlet and a new direction that was completely unexpected. I look forward to what else life has in store for me. Who knows what may around the next bend.

Your Poem

Do you still remember,
We met when we were young?
Lighting an inner spark,
Illuminating our journey that was to come.

A force exists between us,
I don't know I can give a description.
Kindred spirits or pairs,
A force of attraction pulls like gravitation.

We wandered from the light
Of one another, as it is with life sometimes.
We have each had troubles,
Things to work through, falling on hard times.

You feel this connection,
I know this to be true.
Energy draws us together,
You to me and me to you.

This bond we share
Endures as perennial as the seasons.
To deny it's existence
Defies all logic and any good reason.

Until the day comes
That we reunite as is intended,
I wait for you;
Our journey in time remains suspended.

Our souls are pairs,
Made for one another; we are doubles,
To share through time,
Side by side a couple.

Most will never find
The one in this precious lifetime.
To know you're mine
And walk away would be an egregious crime.

When fate's wheel turns
And aligns your path with mine,
We will find each other,
As is intended for the rest of time.

This is my message,
And I send it out to you.
To fight to be together,
Is a struggle that is not new.

We may cause pain
To some in our quest of the heart.
Enduring adversity to find
What has been ours all along from the start.

Party Animal

I have always loved having a good time. I'm all about the party. Did someone say bender? When I feel that urge to go all out, it is like trying to stop a runaway train. Good luck! I will say I have no intention at all to go out partying and bendering once I'm released. It has caused me plenty of trouble over the years, and to go back to my old partying ways would be a poor decision. But the caged animal in me wants to be set free.

I have partied my way through Europe, attending some of the world's biggest music festivals. I've clubbed in Ibiza, run with the bulls in Spain, sailed Croatia. I love a pool party, music festivals, nightclubs, day clubs, and house parties. Wherever the action is happening, that's where I want to be. I love meeting fellow party animals and festival heads on my travels.

I have run into people at a music festival here in Australia that I met partying in a hotel room in Europe. I met two girls from Sydney at Ultra Europe music festival in Croatia who recognised me from Facebook. I made lifelong friends while partying on the gold coast, where although I lived in Sydney, I was considered a local as I was there so regularly. I had regular house parties at my place, which I nicknamed Carry-on Cottage. It became so well known around the area that I had girls at a nightclub whom I had never met ask if I'm the guy who lives in the party cottage.

Anyone who knows me or knows of me will tell you that Scott loves to party. Alcohol, cocaine, and ecstasy go hand in hand with this party lifestyle, and I've consumed more than my fair share of each. It is a load of fun, but it is definitely not good for you and comes with problems. For many years, from about the age of 14 right up until I eventually came to prison for the first time aged 29, partying and having a good time consumed almost all of my time and energy. During that time, I really did not accomplish much else other than enjoying myself.

I worked and paid the bills but made no real progress in any area of my life. There were times when I would experience moments of clarity, thinking to myself that I need to tone it down and start being more responsible and productive. However, I had no real desire to do so, nor the necessary will power to make the changes. I also didn't really know how to live any other way. I wondered what people who didn't party all the time did with their time. Living any other way was a completely alien existence to me. I remember thinking at the time, 'What else can I do? What will I do with myself if I were to quit this party lifestyle?' I didn't come up with much. Stay home and watch movies? BORING! Take up a hobby, perhaps. LIKE WHAT? Will I have to find new friends? But I like my friends. I had no direction and no idea how to live any other way. At the time, I didn't really want to either.

One thing I have learnt and know with absolute certainty is that people will not make changes unless they want to and are ready to, no matter how necessary those changes may seem to anyone else or the trouble being caused by not making them. Of course, that's not to say that we shouldn't raise our concerns to those we care about if they are living and behaving in a way that is causing them or others harm. Raising your concern may well be the catalyst for coming to that decision. If that is what helps them reach the conclusion that change is necessary, then that is a great result, and of course, we should have that discussion. However, until the person reaches that conclusion for themselves, they won't do it. It is often a process that can take a while and a lot of attempts before success.

One upside to all my time in prison is that I have had a lot of time to think long and hard about every aspect of my life and myself. It has allowed me to find my way. It also allowed me to hit the reset button, removing myself from all the habits I was so set in.

As I have discussed, I replaced those habits with new ones for a while, but eventually, I got a handle on it all. Again, change is often a process that can take many attempts.

Nowhere do you have more time for contemplation than in prison. Life in society is so fast paced now. Everyone's schedule is jam packed, with little time spare for anything else outside of their commitments. Work, gym, kids, maintaining the household, school, uni, side hustles, socialising, family commitments, etc. Who has spare time to think in depth constructively, analytically, contemplatively, and philosophically about themselves and the many aspects of their life. Most of our mental energy is spent worrying about work, money, our family, petty dramas, and other people's opinions and perceptions of us.

So how, with all the distractions and time constraints of modern life, can we manage how we spend our mental energy, focusing it towards more constructive and purposeful thought? Meditation.

Meditation has such transformative power, having the ability to change how you think about and view yourself and the world around you. The benefits of meditation are exponential. This point is worth emphasising. You don't even have to know what you are doing. There are guided meditations online that will walk you through it. Once you learn how to meditate, you can start to analyse where your thoughts are focused. This will help to avoid spending mental energy worrying about shit like how others perceive you. You may be surprised what you can learn about yourself just sitting in quiet contemplation.

Despite the rare moments when I thought I ought to change my direction, I never did. The partying continued for me. There is nothing wrong with going out and enjoying yourself, letting off some steam with a big night out here and there. It is a rite of passage growing up, and I would argue it is a normal, healthy part of social interaction.

As we get older, the chances are you probably have less and less interest in having a big night out and have likely had your fill. Plus, hangovers become less and less appealing with age.

To answer the question that I couldn't when I was younger, 'what will I do with myself instead of the partying,' I now have many answers. I'm armed with options. I have so much that I want to achieve that the question now is, 'How will I prioritise my time to fit it all in? How will I find the time? Will one life time even be enough?'

I definitely don't have the desire or time to spend on partying my life away. Looking back, all the partying and good times were about trying to fill a void. I was bored, I had no direction or purpose, and I had no idea what I wanted to do with my life, all of which was making me unhappy. So I filled in my time with as much fun and distraction as possible. Truth being told, I don't entirely regret it all. It would have been nice to figure all this out earlier, without all the prison and hard times, but that's not the way it went for me. Without things turning out the way they did, I wouldn't have learnt the lessons I have or be in the position I am now to share that knowledge. I'm grateful for all my life experiences, the growth and self-development that it has afforded me, and the ability I now have to view it as such. I did have a lot of fun along the way and have met people who have profoundly impacted my life. Who could regret that? That is what this book is all about: what I have learnt from all of my experiences. Isn't that also what life is all about?

'Lessons in life will be repeated until they are learned.'

—Frank Sonnenberg

Party Animal

It's that time again.
I've got the urge to go all out.
A bag of rack,
A bottle or two, come on, it's my shout.

It's a summer day,
Call some girls, we'll party in the pool.
And after dark,
We can hit the town and carry on like fools.

The club is pumping,
The DJ is killing it, and everyone is up dancing.
I give her a smile.
She smiles back; it's time to start romancing.

We share a kiss.
It's loud in here; let's go outside to talk.
We'll grab some drinks.
Bring your friends; the party crew grows some more.

Darkness turns to daylight,
As the sun rises on a brand new day.
But we're still going,
And nowhere near finished yet; no fucking way.

Come back with me.
You're all welcome; the party is still young.
We will do some coke,
Pop some pills, whatever your idea is of fun.

Pump the music loud.
Let's lift the fucking roof off.
This party is cranking.
Let's never stop; pass me another Smirnoff.

It's day two now, I'm having so much fun.
We are full swing into the bender.
I feel so euphoric,
Out of my mind; there will be no surrender.

We will go all day,
We will go all night, the party never dies.
Get more alcohol delivered.
Call the dealer to drop off more supplies.

When we run out of steam,
We will pack things up; but then,
Next time I get the urge,
We'll dust ourselves off and do it all again.

Christmas Day

There is no good time to be in prison. Every day is shit. However, some are worse than others. Christmas and my son's birthdays are the standouts for me. I have spent seven of my own consecutive birthdays in here with one to go at the time of writing. I would much rather be out for them, obviously, but missing my own is not the biggest deal for me. It's missing my son's that hurts the most. Missing parents' and sibling's birthdays are shit as well. Christmas with the family is on par with missing my son's birthday for me. Christmas is a special time of year for the whole family to come together. It's not about gifts but togetherness and celebration. It's nice to give and receive gifts from one another, but the time together is the true gift. Time with family and friends is what is taken from us in prison. That is our real punishment. That is the facet of losing your freedom that really bites.

When first coming into prison, there is a lot to adjust to. Everyone is stressed about money, the legal problems they face, losing the house, the relationship breaking down, losing their job, etc., all of which I have already touched on throughout the book. After a few years have gone by, the court case is over and most of if not all of those above mentioned things are gone, the only thing you still care about losing is time with the ones you love. After the house, money, cars, wife, job, and everything you owned is long gone, it's the lost time that keeps you awake. Material items that once held such value don't seem to be the devastating loss that it felt like at the time. Money can be earned again; houses, cars, even a new wife can all come into your life. You cannot, however, go back and celebrate your child's sixth birthday or redo every Christmas throughout their childhood you missed out on. I came to prison when my son was four years old. He will be twelve once I'm released. That's the real price you pay when you lose your freedom.

I'm not mentioning any of this for sympathy. I don't want nor deserve any. I made poor choices, and this is the cost. I want to convey what it is you're losing by ending up in here.

For the young guys reading this, don't think it's a walk in the park and you're not really losing out because you don't have the kids, house, money, etc. to lose. I have spent time with guys whose parents are terminally ill with cancer and die while they are away. Family members get married and have children. All the friends and girls you spent time with on the outside very quickly forget about you. At first, coming to visit you in gaol is exciting and new, but the novelty wears off fast, and they just stop coming. The world keeps turning, life goes on for everyone else on the outside, and you will find yourself forgotten and left behind. This happens all the time. It's a hard and lonely lesson that almost everyone serving an extended period of time in here learns. People have their own lives, grow up, get married, start families, move away, and move on. It's family who stick by us in the long run and do the time with us. Know the cost of making the mistakes that land you in prison. That is what I want to get across.

I learnt this lesson. I lost everything I had, and people moved on with their lives, as they should. The only thing I care about losing is time with my loved ones who have stuck it out supporting me through over seven tough years. When I think of going home, the image I have in my mind is surrounded by family, sharing a home-cooked meal together. That's all I want.

I wrote this poem on Christmas Day 2021, with ten months remaining on my sentence, determined that this would be the final Christmas I am away from home. Determined that my son wouldn't be opening presents on Christmas morning without his dad around. Adamant there wouldn't be an empty seat around Mum's table at Christmas lunch ever again. I was more sure than I had ever been that I was done with the nonsense that kept landing me in prison, because I didn't ever want to feel like I did again that day. I didn't feel sorry for myself. I have never felt sorry for myself during any of my time incarcerated.

I felt terrible on Christmas Day for everyone I loved and missed, especially my son for having to feel the way he did on each Christmas Day without me around. Each family occasion, birthday, wedding, funeral, Easter, school carnival, weekend sport, and all the other little things – simply just spending time at home together – this is the cost, and not just for the person behind bars. The people at home that stick it out with you serve every single day of that sentence too. If anything, they do it harder.

To live recklessly, live outside the law, not work, do whatever you like, sell drugs, party like a rock star, take what you want when you want, or however it is that people choose to live that lands them in here, along with that choice, know that you are also choosing to cause pain to a great deal of people. Many of those people will be the people closest to you. The ones you love the most will suffer the most. That is a choice you make, whether you admit it or not. It is a fact.

Christmas Day in prison is a shit day. I hate it, and so does everyone else in here. Next year, I can't wait for Christmas Day. I know I will love every minute of that day. I will spend the day surrounded by family, happy that I'm finally able to enjoy Christmas as it should be enjoyed – with the people I love. My son won't have to experience an empty feeling on that day, rather a fulfilled, happy feeling as every kid deserves. No one will have to suffer because of me anymore; rather, they will enjoy themselves with me.

I look forward to being able to support them and being a source of joy and happiness, rather than being a source of stress. This is a choice I'm making now, just as I made a choice to cause pain by living the way I did in the past. Everyone has made the choices they have in order to end up in their current position. Regardless of what that looks like for you, it is true for you as well. At any time, we are all capable of making new choices, and wherever that leads will be on us too.

We are responsible for finding ourselves in our current circumstance. The consequences of our decisions, whether good or bad, are almost always the result of our choices. Of course, there are some unfortunate exceptions, but as a general rule, we create the cause that gives rise to the effect. Once you learn to take responsibility for the choices you are making and the circumstances that they lead to in this way, only then will you be in a position to recognise the cause for the circumstances of today as well as making better choices today to give rise to better circumstances tomorrow.

Merry fuckin' Christmas...

> *'Family, we may not have it all together, but together we have it all.'*
>
> —Unknown

Christmas Day

A special time of year,
To get together with those we love.
Let us celebrate what's good,
Giving thanks for one another, for some to God above.

But for us behind bars,
This day is no cause for celebration.
We spend another year
Missing kids, family, and loved ones due to our incarceration.

There is no one else to blame
But ourselves for being locked up on Christmas Day.
Only it isn't just us suffering,
Children and family bear the brunt while we're away.

On this day, I feel guilt
For letting everyone down who supports me.
An empty feeling each Christmas
My son must suffer because his dad is so naughty.

I seek no sympathy.
I deserve to be punished for my crime.
It's not just me drinking this medicine,
But those I care about are also serving time.

Seven years of Christmas I have missed.
There is nothing festive or joyous about the holiday.
In fact, I hate this time of year.
Without family and friends, I see nothing to celebrate.

They miss me this time of year,
At birthdays and family gatherings too.
Thank God this is my last time.
Next year, I'll be home ready to start anew.

Opening presents with my family,
I can't wait to see the look on everyone's faces.
Just to see you all,
Breakfast, lunch, and dinner visiting everyone's places.

I know next year,
I will love Christmas once again.
It will be as it should be,
Spending the festive season celebrating with family and friends.

Doubt

Doubt is the single biggest obstacle to success. We all have aspirations; we dream about reaching for them and achieving our goals. Often along the way, if not immediately, that negative voice creeps in and starts throwing up obstacles. It starts coming up with reasons it won't work or we can't do it.

For all our intelligence and supposed self-awareness as human beings, often we operate in ways that seem to not make much sense. Our psychology is complex. It seems to me that we find it much easier to take a negative view of ourselves than one of positivity and belief. To point out our shortcomings comes much more easily than to recognise our strengths. If you were asked to write a list of your weaknesses and another of your strengths, most would find the latter much harder, with the list heavy in the weakness column.

I recently wrote a list of my achievements. It was a short list, with nothing new added to it for quite some time. That's not me being negative; it is just a fact. Being in prison long term doesn't exactly lend itself to smashing goals. I decided to write another list. This one was all of the things I want to add to my list of achievements. I set some new goals and thought hard about how I was going to achieve them.

One of the items on this list was to publish a book. I have been writing for a while now; some fiction books are in the works along with this one. If you are reading this book, I obviously achieved my goal, for which I would be extremely grateful. Working on this book at the time of writing has been underway for a couple of years now. When I started writing the poetry, I had no intention of publishing anything or writing a book. The thought of compiling the poems and writing about them came later. At the time, the poetry was just an outlet for me to express the thoughts that were racing around my head. I found it therapeutic. I didn't realise how much was bouncing around up there until I started to put it all on paper. Once I started, I couldn't stop.

Once I did decide that I would compile the poems into a book and had the direction and intention for what I wanted it to be, I noticed that self-doubt rolled in almost immediately. I thought things like, 'I'm not qualified to give an opinion on a lot of the subject matter I touch on. Nobody would be interested to hear someone in prison talking about anything. I don't know the first thing about writing a book,' and plenty of other negative shit. I had started sabotaging myself on the road to achieving my goal at the first step in my journey.

I decided that if I was to achieve any of the goals on my list, I would have to overcome these doubtful thoughts. If I couldn't, I knew I would never succeed. I started to come up with reasons that I could achieve my goals. I set out a plan on how I was going to do it. I knew that negative thoughts would pop up along the way. I knew there would be times I'd experience feelings of self-doubt. I decided when those thoughts did arise, I would counter those thoughts and feelings with positivity. I would tell myself that I am qualified to give an opinion, because I have a wealth of experience. I have dealt with and overcome some serious adversity and emerged the other side. I know what has worked for me has the capacity to be useful for others. What I have to say does have value and will help people. When I tell people what the book is about, they seem genuinely interested, so why wouldn't others be too? People seem interested in what life is like behind prison walls, the life of crime, and the things that lead us to prison.

Once I was armed with my positive thoughts to counter any negativity that came to mind, I was able to quickly and effectively shut it down, allowing me to continue on. I've not lost any confidence since. I will publish this book.

I'm sure that there will be people who criticise me and my views in the book. That's fine. There will always be plenty of people ready to attack you when you put yourself out there. Everyone has an opinion. But I'm resilient enough to stand up to it. There will be enough obstacles that pop up along the way as you strive to achieve your goals. Don't let the negativity of others or your own self-doubt drown out that belief. It will destroy your ambition. Ambition is what got you to set your goals and chase after them in the first place. You don't want to lose it along the way. You will need it to keep the fires of desire burning to succeed.

Persistence, resilience, and belief are the keys to overcoming doubt.

Persistence is required to stay the course over the long run.

Resilience helps you to keep going, despite the setbacks you will inevitably face. After all, nothing worthwhile ever comes easy.

Believe in yourself that you can do it, and you will.

Simple formula. Learn it. Remember it.

It is important to note that having a plan on how you're going to get there is also necessary. A goal without a plan is just a dream, so the saying goes... or something along those lines. Setting small targets to hit along the road to the big goal is an effective tool to keep you motivated. As well as keeping you on track, it gives you something to feel good about with a little taste of success. It breaks down the big goal into smaller, more manageable segments, making the overall task seem less daunting. The rest is hard work. Work hard every single day towards the goal. You will get there.

Paragraph five refers to doubt as a 'pervasive aggressor' that drowns out sense and reason. Once doubt takes hold, it aggressively sets about ruining your goals. Your ambition, belief, and confidence – all necessary to accomplishing your task – are all under attack. As previously stated, these are all the qualities that led you to set your goal in the first place. This can apply to any task you set yourself. It doesn't necessarily have to be a major goal or big dream. It can be anything you strive for. It may be that you want to lose five kilos or work towards a promotion at work. Doubt doesn't care what it is that it sets about ruining; it will take on the task with gusto all the same. If you don't have a game plan on how to overcome doubt as you strive for whatever it is you want to achieve, you are leaving yourself vulnerable. There is a very strong chance that at some point along the way, you're going to have to confront it. It is even likely that you're going to have to deal with it on a recurring basis. Factor it in, be ready to deal with it, and give yourself every opportunity to succeed.

Remember, you have the formula.

'Doubt kills more dreams than failure ever will.'

—Suzy Kassem

Doubt

We all experience doubt,
An enemy we must learn to hurdle.
This imaginary blockade
That can weigh heavily on our dreams; a burden.

Anything worthwhile achieving
Won't come easily; there is always a toll to pay.
Along the road to success,
A thousand obstacles will stand in the way.

To add to this,
We often apply an unnecessary and heavy load.
It is common to think
The task's too much as we walk along that road.

We sabotage ourselves,
An act against the very thing we strive for.
I'll never know why
We allow this vandal to work to keep us poor.

This pervasive aggressor
Can get so loud it drowns out sense and reason.
Destroying ambition from within,
Doubt wins with a successful act of treason.

It is hard enough to win
In life; there is already so much against us.
Let's not doubt ourselves,
Give ourselves a chance to get a few wins up.

Riot! Riot! Riot!

Day-to-day life in prison is generally boring and uneventful. Every now and then, there are confrontations between the inmate and the screws, but it's usually nothing major. Occasionally, tensions boil over completely between inmates and officers. When this happens, things can really escalate. Often, prisoners will express their distain by refusing to follow instructions from correctives staff. The officers will usually then call the squad – IAT (Immediate Action Team). If things aren't quickly defused at this point, a riot can ensue. If the squad can't bring the situation quickly under control, a group called contage are called. Contage is a group much like IAT but is called upon by a prison in situations like a riot to come and take control of the centre and restore order.

Everyone would have seen footage on the nightly news of inmates on prison roofs destroying property and throwing shit at officers. Somehow, when a riot kicks off, there is a news chopper on the scene within minutes. Upon a situation like this kicking off, the prison has protocols that they follow. The staff all run out of the unit, locking everyone in to contain the situation.

Prisons are all segregated into units and yards for this reason. Gone are the days of maximum security prisons being open and everyone being able to mingle with the entire prison population. They have very much applied the divide-and-conquer strategy to gaol layouts. It is much easier for them to control a single contained unit of 60–70 unruly inmates than an entire organised prison population of 600–700. Once the unit is contained, the rest of the prison is locked in cell despite them having nothing to do with the situation. All the officers of the prison now focus on the situation in the problem unit, with many gearing up in riot gear. The officers will try to negotiate with the ring leader (or leaders) or someone appointed as a spokesman for the inmates to bring about a peaceful surrender.

The officers will usually make promises to address whatever the issue was that caused the blow up in the first place, promises that they will never keep. Failing that, they will then make threats to strip inmates of privileges and lock everyone in for an extended period of time, which is going to happen regardless once things have reached this point. Knowing all this, the prisoners will usually tell them to go and get fucked, so the screws go about planning to take the unit back by force.

This is when things really kick off.

It may sound exciting, but when they fire a dozen gas canisters into the unit and empty a few large cans of capsicum spray in the mix, it gets a lot less fun very quickly. I doubt too many of you reading this would have had any exposure to tear gas or pepper spray, but let me tell you from having had multiple experiences with both chemicals, individually and in combination, it fucking sucks. I don't recommend it at all.

Despite looking all exciting and interesting watching it unfold on the news, this is what it is actually like being in a prison riot.

Once the gas is fired, it is almost impossible to get a breath of air in. Your airways close up, while simultaneously filling up with snot and mucus. Your eyes, skin, and airways burn horribly. You naturally panic because you can't breathe, and your brain is screaming at you that you're going to die. So you and everyone around you have a simultaneous panic attack. Any fight you had in you is now gone. The only thing you care about is getting oxygen. Your entire existence is reduced to and focused on getting in a breath of air. But it's not over at this point; things have only just begun.

Now, the squad and contage run, in storming the yard. They are completely unaffected by the chemicals with their gas masks and gear on. They have angry attack dogs that want nothing more than to tear off your calf muscle. They have extendable batons and shields and are often pumping more and completely unnecessary amounts of chemicals into the air.

Their sole intention at this point is to fuck everyone up. They will say that is not true and that their only aim is to quickly bring the situation under control. That is a load of shit. This is a good time to the officers of the squad and contage. They have free reign to get away with punishing us without any recourse.

Anyone who has ever suffered a panic attack will tell you that it is a horrible experience. Try to imagine having one while not being able to breathe from the effects of the gas, while your eyes, skin, and airways burn from the chemicals, a vicious attack dog barking inches from your face while very angry riot squad officers beat the shit out of you. Still, the only thing you care about is air. Any small amount of air you do manage to take in while all this is going on is filled with more poison. Finally, you're handcuffed or cable tied and dragged to your cell and locked in, still covered in all the chemicals. That is essentially what it is like being involved in a riot. And you will likely spend weeks locked in cell afterwards.

It very rarely, if ever, achieves a favourable outcome for the inmates. But when everyone is consumed by boredom, using drugs, frustrated, stressed, and on edge, it is unavoidable. It is an inevitable pressure release valve. It wouldn't come as any shock to anyone that sometimes, the screws can be real arseholes towards inmates, which is often the catalyst. All it takes is a small amount of provocation to the wrong person on the wrong day, and things can really kick off. Things can escalate very quickly, and everyone just jumps on the bandwagon. Often, when this happens, anyone who doesn't want to get involved will be threatened by the others. The option is to face the wrath of the screws or the other inmates.

Prison politics is complicated. Sometimes, you don't have a choice. The screws know this but don't care. You'll be punished all the same.

'A riot is the language of the unheard.'

—Martin Luther King

Riot! Riot! Riot!

Riot! Riot! Riot!
We're not copping your shit today.
Riot! Riot! Riot!
Fuck the screws; we're taking over Long Bay.

You've pushed us to our limit.
We're not animals; this time, you have gone too far.
Today we make our stand.
Bring it on; we want war in the yard.

Here comes the squad.
Don't back down lads; we have to stand our ground.
They'll come in hard.
We will give 'em hell; what a medieval sound.

Like old colonial soldiers,
They line up outside the fence for battle.
We stick staunch together,
Cornered in the yard herded up like cattle.

They fire in gas canisters,
Attack dogs bark while we prepare to defend.
Pepper spray fills the air,
Outgunned and outnumbered, we are in it until the end.

We send fire back,
Slingshotting the canisters with our shirts.
This has little effect.
They have masks; the beating we'll cop will hurt.

It's impossible to breathe.
We've been attacked with chemical warfare.
Everyone is buckled over.
The fight drained right out of us as we struggle for air.

It's all over quite quickly.
They flood in taking over the yard.
We're shown no mercy.
Dying for oxygen, still they beat on us hard.

Although we've been defeated,
We hold pride in a small moral victory.
They think we'll just cop their shit.
Next time, they'll think twice before they try to fuck with me.

Treat us poorly again,
And we will muster the troops once more.
Next time, we might attack first.
Fuck around again, and be weary when opening the cell door.

Ambivalence

Ambivalence in a nutshell means having conflicting thoughts, emotions, or feelings about something. Here, I use it to express the feeling of being torn between making changes in my life for the better or staying on the course I was on. The psychological tug-of-war a lot of us experience when faced with change, the internal conflict we feel before making that choice, that's ambivalence.

This feeling of ambivalence is commonly experienced by people with drug and alcohol issues who recognise the need to make changes in their lives around the problem but struggle with tackling the addiction. Another good example would be feeling torn between staying in a bad relationship and leaving. Despite knowing it's doing harm to stay and being miserable, the fear of leaving what is familiar for the unknown is terrifying.

For me, in the poem, I'm describing making the necessary changes around the party lifestyle I was living, leaving behind the people in my life who were dragging me down and other lifestyle choices that kept landing me in trouble. By this stage in the book, you would have noticed that there is a fair bit of crossover between many of the topics we have discussed. In an earlier chapter, I touched on peoples fear of change, and now here it is again. That's what ambivalence really boils down to. That internal conflict felt, is fear of change. We know the change is what's best for us but we are scared to jump. The fear of the unknown over what we know for certain, despite what we know and are familiar with being shit.

For anyone who has had, or knows anyone who has had, issues with any kind of addiction, whether drugs, alcohol, gambling, or whatever else, you would be aware that the person going through it will believe that they have a handle on things or that there is no problem at all.

I've heard regular ice users come up with all sorts of reasons that they could stop anytime they like or that they just choose not to and don't have a problem.

Alcoholics will say that they work hard so they deserve to drink each night when they get home; it helps them sleep. Their justification is that if they did have a problem, they couldn't function and go to work each day.

I've heard the exact same argument from cocaine addicts regarding working, except they can't sleep without taking Xanax or Valium, which becomes another addiction.

None of this means you don't have a problem. It just means you manage to function along with the issue. Functioning addict is the term commonly used. It is often a short step between functioning and non-functioning.

Recognising there is an issue and you're not in control is the first step. I have never participated in AA or NA meetings, but this is the first step in that 12-step program/system. There is no way a problem can be addressed if the person with the issue doesn't accept that they have one. This goes for any issue someone has.

Take addiction and criminal offending completely out of the picture. Let's say someone's problem is that they are overweight and very unhealthy. They eat a lot of fast food, drink sugar-filled soft drinks all day long, are carrying plenty of body fat, and are obviously unfit and easily become short of breath from the most minimal amount of activity. It may be blindingly obvious to everyone around them that they could definitely do with losing a few kilos and keep a much better diet. If this person doesn't believe they need to lose any weight and their diet is fine, then there is zero chance of that situation changing for them. This is a common issue with the current PC, woke nonsense messaging around body positivity that makes it acceptable and even encourages and celebrates poor health. If someone wants to be overweight and unhealthy, that's fine. It's their life to live how they see fit. But I strongly disagree with the positive messaging around it.

To me, that would be the same as positive messaging around smoking cigarettes. We know the harmful health effects of smoking, so advertising was banned as a result. The harm done to the body as a result of obesity and the unhealthy lifestyle choices that cause it are on par. Yet, we are supposed to embrace it under the banner of body positivity. It's nonsense. Again, I'm all for people living however they choose to live, but we should make those choices knowing all the facts and consequences we face as a result. Why shouldn't we be able to call a spade a spade and speak to the truth of any matter? So long as we do so with respect and the right intent, I don't think there should be any issue.

It took a while for me to come around to accepting that my lifestyle choices had to change. Like many people do, I came to this point by hitting rock bottom when the consequences all came to bear. For those people who are extremely overweight and unhealthy, those consequences usually come to bear in the form of a heart attack, stroke, developing diabetes, etc. In my case, it was being shot, almost dying, and coming back to prison again. I had thought about the need to change my ways in the past. I had thought about it seriously. It wasn't as though I wasn't already aware of the issue itself and the problems being caused as a result. It was under the weight of the unbearable consequences in the situation I was in that my hand was forced to act.

In the past, ambivalence pulled me back, believing I could work around the issue, essentially having my cake and eating it too. This time, I couldn't bargain my way out of change.

At the time of writing this poem, I had already made a clear determination and commitment to doing the work on myself and sorting out the issues. The poem is a reflection back to the time when I was struggling with ambivalence. Looking back at that time from my current position of clarity, it seems like utter madness to try to bargain with myself, believing that I was capable of being in control of it all. At the time, though, I was delusional enough to believe my own bullshit. Just the same as the overweight and unhealthy person pretends they are happy and there is no need to change anything under the body positivity banner, I too was able to convince myself that it was all fine. If we can't be honest with ourselves and each other and speak truthfully to an issue, then we will just keep living in delusion. Because on the other side of that honesty and tough conversation, we can effect positive change.

Life has so much good to offer once we are able to lift the veil of delusion and work towards a better self. I've never met anyone who has overcome addiction who has told me that sobriety is a worse way to live. It may not be easy, but it's worth the struggle. I'm yet to meet someone who has overcome obesity and now lives a healthy and balanced lifestyle who regrets the change and doesn't feel much better and happier within themselves. Have you? I very much doubt it.

Ambivalence will make a liar out of all of us if we allow it. We convince ourselves and try to convince others of our bullshit. Regardless of whatever it is we experience internal conflict over, being honest with ourselves is the only path to making the right choice. It's not easy being honest with yourself and facing up to your problems. Often, hitting rock bottom and being forced when faced with the consequences of our choices is the only way it occurs. It's usually then in that vulnerable state that we drop our ego, which is built on a foundation of our own bullshit and inflated self-image. Now, we can honestly look at ourselves and are in a position to make real change. It may be a long and tough road to travel towards a better you or set of circumstances, but it's only from a position of honesty with yourself can you start along that road. Until then, you will forever be stuck on the ambivalence merry-go-round, going nowhere fast.

> *'Things may come to those who wait, but only the things left by those who hustle.'*
>
> —Abraham Lincoln

Ambivalence

I recognise the need to change.
It won't be easy, but I can't go on like this.
For too long now,
Something in my life has been amiss.

I've tried in the past
To turn my back on my destructive ways.
Something always pulls me back,
A devil on the shoulder convincing me to stay.

So I begin planning
On how I will weather the storm.
I've got it this time.
You will hold sway over me no more.

Once I reach that precipice,
I begin to bargain with the problem within.
I can control it this time.
The caged animal is free; once again, it wins.

I want better for myself.
There is a brand-new life waiting for me.
If only I could manage
To overcome ambivalence, I would finally be free.

This internal tug-of-war continues.
I hope this time I can enjoy victory.
My persistence pays off,
So all of life's good things can make their way to me.

This Is Me

The quote at the end of this chapter by Oscar Wilde, 'Be yourself, everyone else is taken,' is a favourite of mine. It's short and simple but is jam-packed with a wealth of wisdom. Nothing or no one will ever rob you of more than trying to live as anyone other than who you are as a person, whether that's trying to fit in to a social group, attempting to please another or others by moderating your speech, behaviour, appearance, views, opinions, beliefs, or who you are as a human being.

To try to fit someone else's mould or to meet expectations of what or who they think we ought to be comes at great personal cost. The price you'll pay is everything you are, everything you believe in, your strength and happiness. You will have to compromise your values. You'll forfeit your free will and free thinking. You will second guess your own thoughts and emotions, seeking validation and verification from others that it's ok to think and feel the way you do. Bit by bit, you lose a piece of yourself until there is nothing left.

Others will always have an opinion about how we ought to live, think, even feel about things. This occurs at a societal level, within institutions, and in relationships. Often, there will be threats and consequences that play on our fears for noncompliance. For example, the church will tell you to live within the prescribed guidelines in the bible, or else you will go to hell.

If you voice an opinion publicly that doesn't align with accepted societal norms, you'll be cancelled. Free speech shouldn't be conditional on the views being voiced aligning with what is deemed acceptable by others. Yet, that is what's occurring with the current cancel culture in western society.

The problem with this type of woke approach to silencing anyone not in agreeance is that it stifles debate and open conversation on anything in the slightest bit controversial.

Politicians are more interested in trying to keep everyone happy and appear squeaky clean over actually putting forward good policy for fear of opening themselves up for attack.

Media outlets run the same type of stories around the same type of opinions and don't conduct actual impartial investigative journalism on a wide range of topics that would allow us to form our own informed opinions based on unbiased fact. They don't want to lose advertising dollars, so they must remain within the confines of what is socially acceptable. Staying within those lines becomes harder and harder as they become ever narrower.

The point I'm getting to with this is that if you try to live this way trying to please others, staying within the boundaries of what others expect of you, it will come with great sacrifice. Just as our politicians have sacrificed any ability to effectively do their job, just as the media have sacrificed their integrity as journalists and the ability to convey unbiased information, you too will sacrifice your voice and happiness in an attempt to live to please. You'll live silently in fear of upsetting whoever it is you're trying to appease.

How often have you witnessed a friend or family member in a toxic relationship, allowing themselves to be controlled or coerced into modifying their behaviour in some way to suit their partner? They aren't allowed out anymore, they dress differently, they may not be allowed to spend or even have access to money. A vibrant, happy, social individual becomes quiet and withdrawn. I have seen this happen with both men and women. There is a difference between healthy compromise in a relationship and control.

Perhaps you have found yourself looking back on one of your own past relationships wondering why on earth you allowed yourself to live under something akin to a dictatorship. No one should sacrifice their own freedom to be in relationship. A relationship should improve and enrich your life.

Often, for someone in one of these relationships, they become enslaved forever trying to please their partner. Rather than the relationship enriching their life, they end up robbed of everything good in it. They end up a shell of their former self, having compromised their values and given up their independence and happiness to satisfy often narcissistic expectations in an unwinnable battle.

To be true to who you are and living authentically to your own set of beliefs and values is to be free and happy in your own skin. You can speak openly and honestly without fear on any subject you wish. You will never feel the need to moderate your speech when voicing an opinion to appease your audience. Your strong spirit will show through in your personality rather than been suffocated out of you in silence. You will act with conviction and purpose because you are full of confidence and self-belief. You know who you are and what you stand for. You are not concerned with the opinions of others about who you are or what you do. Any changes or self-improvement you make is undertaken on your own terms for your own reasons. If anyone were ever to try to tear you down or pull you back into line, you'd push back hard, stand tall, and tell 'em, 'I am who I am. I won't ever bend or break. I won't change for you or anyone else. Like it or not, this is me.'

> 'Those that were seen dancing were thought to be insane by those who could not hear the music.'
>
> —Friedrich Nietzsche

This Is Me

To change who you are,
Appeasing others, is only living a lie.
The spirit in you,
Day by day, a little piece of it dies.

We are who we are.
There is nothing worth fitting someone else's mould.
You will always be enslaved,
Serving another until you're miserable and old.

I am who I am,
Not for you or any other will I ever bend.
No matter the cost,
I won't change me; my own man until the end.

You will find yourself asking,
'How on earth did I get into this mess?'
Living to keep others happy
Will come at the expense of your own happiness.

If you make changes,
Be sure it is for your own reasons.
For growth and self-betterment,
Not to suit the crowd, changing with the seasons.

Stand tall and proud
When looking at the reflection in the mirror.
Who you are is enough.
You can be a champion, a stone-cold killer.

People will always have an opinion
And expectations of what we ought to be.
Don't ever be afraid
To speak up; tell 'em, 'Like it or not, this is me.'

Dark Days

Depression, melancholy, self-loathing, rock bottom. I've experienced many dark days while in prison. Sometimes, it's just a bad day missing home, my son, family, or just over being in this shit place. Other times, it has lasted weeks and months. Although I am writing about depression in general, when I wrote the poem, I had a specific time in mind when I returned to prison on this most recent occasion.

That period of time during those first few months of the sentence I am currently serving were tough. I was deeply depressed. I was suffering on a personal, spiritual, psychological, and physical level. I was fucked. I felt fucked worse than I have ever felt in my life. I hated myself so much. I hated that I had hurt my family again by coming back to prison. I had broken my promise to never return almost immediately after been released for my previous offence. I was a broken man.

Looking back at that time now, I'm grateful for that immense suffering. From that place, the lowest of all lows, I was able to start rebuilding myself. A complete overhaul from the bottom up to build a better and stronger version of myself.

Any strong building needs good foundations to stand up to the stress and weight it will be exposed to. It needs to be able to stand up to extreme weather and adverse conditions. There can be no weak spots in the foundation. No matter how strong the structure may be, if the foundations are weak, the building will crumble under stress. The same is true of each of us. Without a strong foundation built of values, self-awareness, and resilience, we too will crumble under pressure and adverse conditions.

Starting from that place, completely broken down, stripped of my ego, with nothing but the hard truth and severe consequences of my actions, I was forced to start working on myself, foundations up. I had no idea how to do that. I had no answers. I just made a commitment to working it out so I would never put my family and loved ones through it all ever again. Despite being lost on how to go about finding the answers I was looking for, I was able to start asking myself the right questions.

When you get to the point where you're asking yourself the right questions, then you can start finding the answers you need. Asking yourself tough questions and being honest with yourself is the beginning of self-growth and betterment. From there, it's a tough slog with a lot of hard work, but you're on your way.

Some of questions I started with were:

- Have I been a good father to my son?
- What type of father do I want to be?

- Am I willing to do the work so I'm not in this position again?
- Am I capable of being better than I have been?
- What do I want out of life?
- Am I happy with how have been living up until this point?

I didn't like some of the answers I came up with, which was strong motivation to start doing better. Being honest with yourself can be really difficult. It is a big part of the reason we often don't like to face the truth and own up to our short falls. Asking myself if I have been a good father to my son and coming up with no was tough.

I had been in prison for most of his life. When I was out, I was busy partying having and a good time, and much of the time I did spend with him, I was tired and hungover. I wasn't happy with how I had lived my life up until that point. I felt like I hadn't really achieved anything, which was also a shit feeling.

I was already really depressed for letting my family down by coming back to prison. I was facing big charges and knew I would be here for a long time. Coming to these realisations after asking myself all these tough questions at this time was such a kick in the guts when I was already down for the count.

However, it needed to happen. To go back to the building foundations analogy, it was like demolishing a derelict structure and starting from scratch. I needed to dig deep, shine a light on every aspect of myself that needed work, and address it altogether.

When I talk about my foundations, what exactly am I addressing? My values. To me, my values are the core of who I am and what I stand for. What type of man am I? What's most important to me?

Things like been a good father; being family orientated; being honest, reliable, and trustworthy; showing compassion for others; being generous and kind; being a good friend; acting with good intention.

To be a good father, I knew I needed to sort my shit out, stay away from drugs and alcohol, and get out of prison and stay out. I needed to work on the issues that were at the heart of and casual to the drug and alcohol use and repeatedly coming to prison.

In addition to that work, I also started setting goals to work towards a better future for myself. Having something to strive for, to have hope of achieving it, and to keep busy working towards is therapeutic in itself.

Depression is ugly. We all get down from time to time, but being really depressed is something different. It can seem an impossible task to see anything good beyond whatever you're going through. All of your thinking is negative and self-defeating. You feel physically as well as mentally drained. Even small problems feel insurmountable, and any level of resilience to deal with them is lost to you.

As harsh or controversial as it may seem, it is a choice whether you remain in this state of mind or turn it around. At any time, you can choose to drop the victim mentality and start constructively working on addressing the issue. This is not to say that you will miraculously feel great all of a sudden; you may feel no better at all for some time. But upon making that switch to a positive mindset, one conducive to problem solving and positive action, you'll be on your way to better days.

There is every chance that you will start to feel better, because you can begin to see your way out. You can start feeling hope for that better day and a return to happiness. You have to develop the strength to pull yourself up and out of it. You have to build resilience. I have already spoken on developing mental toughness and resilience throughout the book. When you work on these core values when times are good, they come in very handy during tough times. Adversity is a great time to begin developing these qualities for those who haven't. You will come out the other side stronger than ever, hardened for the experience and ready for what comes next... only if you make the choice to view it as such. Until then, you will always be the victim, feeling as though life is unfairly hard on you, destined forever to be stuck going round and round on that merry-go-round.

Every day, make a conscious choice to be happy, and you will be. Choose to work hard on yourself, developing your core values and strengths. Choose to exercise, do a cold plunge, strive for something hard to achieve, learn something new, or do something charitable. Take positive action to work on a weakness to turn it into a strength.

Know that this is how strong, successful, high achieving, and happy individuals get to where they are. They choose a positive outlook. They work hard towards improving themselves and their position.

The same is true for everyone else on the other side of that coin. You have made choices each and every day to be where you are. Once you can recognise and accept this concept, you can start making new, better choices to start moving in a new direction, whatever direction you so choose.

We all make hundreds if not thousands of decisions every day: what to eat, what to wear, what we are going to do on the weekend, what show to watch, to go to the gym or not, which way to go, what time to go to bed, etc. You also choose to be happy or not about something, whether you are offended or not, whether you react in anger or not. It's all a choice. So take responsibility for your choices. Choose to be happy and enjoy life, and you will. Choose a positive mindset over the negative, and watch life change for the better for you.

As our New Zealand neighbours would say, 'Choice, bro.'

Dark Days

Dark clouds roll in.
I feel the storm brewing within.
Weighed down so heavily,
As the melancholy and gloom sets in.

Often, it feels like
Being stuck at the bottom of a deep, dark well.
Looking up from the shadows,
A faint light high above from down in this hell.

Happiness seeming impossible,
Like swimming an ocean full of hungry sharks.
The negativity is all-consuming,
The black dog has such a loud viscous bark.

It can be so hard
To see a way out when enveloped by the fog.
But the sun will shine,
Lifting the cloud revealing your path to the top.

Life is a roller coaster.
You have to ride the ups and downs.
So pick yourself up,
Dust yourself off, and prepare for another round.

Know that dark days end,
As sure as the day follows night.
You will see your way through,
Stay the course, and make it back into the light.

Diamond Life

I grew up in the suburbs of western Sydney around Penrith. My family weren't ever poor but were certainly not well off. I would describe our family of six as the typical working-class family. I am the eldest of four kids, Dad was a truck driver, and Mum worked as a checkout attendant. The whole area was typically working class. Everyone got by; no one was well off. Crime was common around the area. Police raided homes and carted people off to gaol. Everyone had an older brother, friend, a cousin, Dad or uncle who was in a bike club, in prison or sold drugs. It was these guys who drove nice cars, rode Harley-Davidson motorbikes, wore expensive jewellery, and pulled out large wads of cash at the bar. They had gorgeous women hanging off them, and everyone showed them respect. It seemed as though they were local celebrities. To a young guy without a dollar to his name and pissed off at the world for his shitty position in it, it seemed like a dream life. That's the allure.

I remember wondering how do they pull women like that. I want that kind respect from people. I want that lifestyle. I want that money. These guys were big, strong, heavily tattooed, dangerous-looking people. They wore thick gold chains, gold watches, were well dressed, and drove nice cars. They would walk into a restaurant, club, or bar, and everyone would want to shake their hands, buy them a drink, and show them respect. In my mind, this is what success looked like.

I started lifting weights in my teens, I was always a skinny kid and wanted to put on some size for football and to attract women. It was also common to run into trouble around the area, the local shops, or train station especially. The pubs were violent places too, once I was old enough to get in. Having a bit of muscle was handy.

The local gym I started training at when I was a teenager was owned at the time by the president of the local OMCG chapter. The guys who worked out there were massive, all obviously on steroids. It wasn't long before I also started using steroids and began packing on some muscle too. It gave me a lot of confidence. I was strong, and it felt good to look in the mirror and see strength. I started to get some attention from women, which helped my confidence as well.

One of the side effects of steroid use can be aggression, and I got a good dose of it. I was always fighting when I went out. The areas pubs and clubs were always violent, so for a juiced up, drunk, and angry young man, trouble was never hard to find. What made things worse was that I liked it. I wanted to fight. I loved the feeling of anger, aggression, and rage, adrenaline pumping and dishing out punishment. A few times, I got beaten up, but I didn't care. It was all part of the fun. To many people, a fight is a once or twice in a lifetime event, if at all. To me, it was a normal part of enjoying a night out.

I was young, big, strong, full of steroids, and violent. I became exactly the type of guy that bike clubs want to recruit. Bike clubs, gangs, criminal groups, etc. rely upon and grow on portraying a strong image. It is everything to them. If they appear to be weak in any way, they will quickly decline. Weakness will be exploited, and others will move in and take their business, rip them off, take them on, and run them out of town. Strength attracts strength. If a group is seen to be strong, it will attract new members of good calibre.

Strength, power, and money all go hand in hand. With the big money involved in this lifestyle, it quite literally pays to be the strongest group. Violence, intimidation, and fear are currency. It acts as a strong deterrent against anyone who might want to take you on to know they face a very tough enemy. Hence, these groups are always looking to bring in new blood who can bolster that image. A young violent man the way I was fit the bill perfectly, and they sought to bring me on board.

They do this by showing young guys a good time, inviting them to their clubhouse nights, and taking them out. Strip clubs, dinners, and parties. They flash cash and have plenty of attractive women around. They talk of a close-knit group where everyone looks out for one another. They call it a brotherhood where everyone gets looked after. They promise that if you come on board, you too will be looked after, and everything they have, you can have too. To young guys who grow up without much, looking up to guys like this is a very attractive proposal. It seems too good to be true, like you've hit the jackpot.

The party lifestyle is a lot of fun. Having money for the first time in your life is great. Having lots of women around and interested in you is everything a young man dreams of. Of course, it all comes at a price.

That strength and violence that was so attractive to the group is your value to them. Your ability to make them money and protect their money is your value. You must constantly prove your worth again and again. It doesn't end. You are a foot soldier. You will follow orders from people who, despite their promises, don't give a fuck about you. Like soldiers, you're disposable and replaceable. Like soldiers, people die.

With all the fighting and shit that comes with the lifestyle, hospital, prison, and graves are likely destinations. Not many people get through unscathed. Everyone who lives this lifestyle goes to prison at some point, and people do die. What seemed so great in the beginning becomes ugly very quickly. Violence between groups erupts, and police start raiding houses, making arrests, and carting people off to prison. People you thought were friends, a part of the so-called brotherhood, cooperate with the police and testify against their own.

No one sees it coming, but it happens regularly. Once in prison and serving your sentence, the guys in the group who aren't in prison quickly forget about you, because you're no longer valuable to them. They look to recruit new blood to continue to support the groups image, maintain control, and make them money. You'll spend all your money on legal fees until you have nothing left.

If you own a house, cars, motorbikes, etc., it all goes too. If the police or crimes commission don't seize it, the lawyers or ex-wife will take it all. Most guys get out of prison with nothing.

It's the price we pay. If you want to play this game, know that this scenario is highly likely. It is a shit experience, but it's only half of the picture; it's not even the worst half of it.

The violence goes both ways. It's naïve to believe that your crew is the only side capable of getting the other. You put yourself, your family, and anyone close to you in danger when you live this life. Gone are the days when the family home and the family themselves are off limits. Homes are invaded and shot up, family members threatened, assaulted, kidnapped, even murdered to punish you. Your friends around you start getting killed, and you find yourself attending funerals. You see the pain and suffering the families endure as a result: young children now fatherless, partners widowed, parents burying sons. This is the true cost of a life of crime. It's the families who pay that bill. We go to prison and die, while they are left to deal with the consequences. Your parents, partner, children, and family will all suffer immensely, because you wanted to act like a gangster. However hard the consequences are for you to bear and tough to go through, they have it tougher. That's what you are choosing when you live this lifestyle. It's selfish, reckless, and dangerous for you and everyone you care about. It all seems great until the inevitable harsh realities start hitting home.

Watching children scared, sad, and confused while their father's coffin is lowered is an experience I never wish to have again.

I didn't write this book to tell anyone how they should or shouldn't live their lives. If someone wants to go down this path, then go for it. It's your life to fuck up how you see fit, but do so knowing the cost.

If after reading about the consequences of it all and weighing it up, you believe somehow that it doesn't apply to you, that's fine.

I would say the only way you will ever come to the same conclusions I have is finding out for yourself. The hard way, just as I had to. For many, that's the only way they'll ever learn life's lessons. It's a tough road for you and everyone around, you but that's your decision to make.

I wrote the book with the intention to share my experiences and what I've learnt on this tough journey with the view of being of benefit to others in the hope that they don't have to repeat my mistakes while shedding some light on what is like to walk in these shoes. Here's what I have learnt about this chapter's subject.

The reason it all seemed too good to be true to the younger version of me was that it was. From the outside looking in, it all appears fantastic; however, it is anything but. To the young guys who grow up without much and especially with shit family and home situations, the allure of money, brotherhood, and belonging is hard to resist. That respect I thought I saw being afforded to these guys was fear. People living this lifestyle think they are respected. People will show you respect out of fear, but they don't actually have a shred of respect for you. If anything, they think very little of you. This is proven when everything goes to shit for you, when you look around to see who is still supporting you and standing by your side, and they are nowhere to be seen.

When you're promised that you'll be looked after and you'll be a part of the brotherhood, you're being sold a dream that doesn't exists. It's a sales tactic that works quite well. Anything you gain living this way, you'll lose, and what it costs will be 100 times the loss. Time and life can't be regained. Not just your own life, but the life of others. It's a deadly game that some just don't make it out of.

You'll experience and cause a lot of pain and suffering that far outweighs any joy you'll get out of it. The lessons you learn along the way are hard ones. Some will break you no matter how hard you think are. At some point, you too will come to the same realisations that I have. You'll have a tough slog ahead of you to get your life back on track while attempting to mend the damage you've done along the way. Some damage, you'll find, can't be undone, no matter how much you try. What appeared to be the diamond life turns out to be a dog's life. Who'd ever choose that?

> *'Things are not always what they seem; the first appearance deceives many; the intelligence of a few perceives what has been hidden.'*
>
> —Phaedrus

Diamond Life

When I was young,
I looked up to some guys from the area.
They wore gold chains,
Looked very tough, and money was no barrier.

They drove expensive cars,
Women on their arms, and started riding motorbikes.
I wanted what they had,
This diamond life that they lived, I liked.

Growing up in Sydney's west,
No one had much money.
So to see these guys
Living this lifestyle seemed as sweet as honey.

I got drawn in
By this mirage; they said that they would look after me.
I made some cash,
I gained respect, and life was a party.

But with the good
Comes the bad, the drama, and the violence.
We went to work,
Living by our code, fear ensuring people's silence.

Gangsters doing what they do,
War erupting in the streets.
Urban soldiers follow orders,
Fighting for control from west to Sydney's east.

Police made their moves,
The public will not accept this mayhem.
Task force raptor
Smashing down our doors to put it to an end.

Courtrooms and prison
Are only half of all the strife.
As with any war,
Some pay the price with their life.

Attending another funeral,
You have to ask yourself the question.
Is any of this worth it?
The casket lowers, and I look at his children's expression.

Nothing could ever justify
The cost of this deadly business.
Not money or power,
I'm finished with it, I swear God as my witness.

Going Home

Getting out of prison is an amazing feeling. The day of release has been the focus of so much of your energy and attention for months and years. It feels as though you are counting down to the biggest day of your life. Everything you want and plan for the rest of your life is dependent on this day coming around. Life can finally recommence after being on hold for so long.

It is both stressful and a source of relief all at once. It's excitement, joy, and happiness with a healthy dose of anxiety. It's many emotions all rolled into one, but it's good. Finally, on the morning of your release date, your name is called to head up to reception to go home. Just hearing your name called triggers a big dump of endorphins. The friends you've spent so much time with stuck in this shitty place together get around you to send you off, wishing you all the best. Everyone's happy that your day has come around.

The screws come and collect you and walk you up to reception to start the release process. Removing the shitty prison greens and putting on your own civilian clothing feels like shedding an uncomfortable skin. It is so refreshing and such a good feeling to be wearing your own clothing again, wearing your own shoes – the clothes of a free man rather than a prisoner. It is the first moment of feeling free, feeling like a human being again.

Walking towards the main gate with your release paperwork in hand, wearing your own civilian clothing is so exciting. The anticipation has reached a crescendo, feeling like your heart will burst out of your chest. When that gate opens and you take that first step out into the free world, it is all behind you. All the stress, uncertainty, waiting, boredom, day-to-day problems, drama, politics, missing family and home, living like a fucking caged animal locked in a cell, it's done.

What's in front of you is all that matters now – your family standing there to greet you. The rest of your life awaits with open arms.

The two times I have been released, I have had family waiting outside the gates to greet me, which was nice. To step outside into the arms of loved ones is everything I had dreamt of when I had envisaged my release dates. To hug my son, Mum, and brother, seeing the joy on their faces – especially my little son – was a special moment that I will never forget. I look forward to that moment again, hopefully for the last time. That moment comes off the back of a great deal of hardship for them, and I never want to be the cause of that kind of pain and suffering to anyone ever again.

Along with the joy of being reunited with family and finally being out of prison comes the opportunity for a fresh start. The feeling of a new beginning with a clean slate is a good one. To leave all the past troubles behind, having paid your debt to society and have another chance, is a good feeling. Sometimes, coming to prison is the necessary circuit breaker an individual needed to break the cycle they were in. Prison was the reset button required to start over, and being released is the opportunity to get everything back on track. Taking that first step out of the gate feels like the first step on that journey.

While in custody, we have so much spare time to think. We dream of the day when we are out and can do all the things we want to do and all that we want to achieve. For some, it's getting back to a normal work routine and a normal life, spending time with the family or starting one of their own. For others, it's starting a business or working towards buying a house. Some people's dreams are less productive; they just want to get out to party with their mates and chase women.

Regardless, everyone gets out with a plan, and it's exciting to finally get out and have the opportunity to make it a reality.

It may seem odd that we feel stressed and anxious about getting out. However, almost everyone who has spent an extended period of time locked up experiences this. Being released comes with a lot of pressure and high expectations.

For me, the anxiety around being released is about not letting down the people who had supported me – my son and family along with a few close friends. I know I can't afford to fuck things up again. I have to make things work on the outside for good this time. My repeated incarcerations have had a devastating effect on those close to me, especially my son. They have suffered a great deal of hardship because of my poor choices. I no longer want to be the cause of stress, disappointment, and pain to my loved ones.

I feel the weight of their and my own expectations to succeed once I'm released. I want better for myself. I want better for them.

Another source of anxiety for guys being released is attempting to fit back into society. Going from a structured prison environment to freedom can be a difficult transition. Losing that routine and structure leaves many who have had it so long feeling lost. Leaving a familiar environment where you know who everyone is and going out in the open public full of strangers is unnerving. We are used to constantly assessing threats in prison, with an underlying tension ready at any time for things to turn ugly. New faces are another potential threat. For someone just released from custody after a lengthy sentence, a trip to a shopping centre can feel overwhelming. A very busy open space full of strange faces sends that threat assessment response into overdrive. It may seem odd that someone coming out of an extremely volatile, violent environment would feel uncomfortable in a shopping centre.

Often, men released from custody will say that they feel more at ease in a prison yard than in public for a period of time. Society and freedom itself, although being the very thing we long for throughout our sentence, is a cause of anxiety when we have to face it.

Some can't handle it and will reoffend with the intention of being caught to return to prison. These people are institutionalised, often having been in and out of custody from a young age and not knowing any other way of living. In fact, it is common for long termers to return under these circumstances. Some don't want to get out, at all; they are scared of the outside world and are much more comfortable in prison.

For the majority of us, though, feeling anxious about getting out is just about the anticipation and big build up to the day. It has been a long time coming, and we can't wait to get started on living the rest of our lives.

The moment when you pull into your street and see home for the first time is epic. At that point, it's all over. You're finally home. It signifies the end of the horrendous journey you have endured. You have taken the final step and crossed the finish line. It takes some time for it all to seem real. I felt like it could have been a dream and that I may just wake up back in my cell at any moment. On many occasions in prison, I had dreams where I was home or free out in society, only to be disappointed to wake up realising it was just a dream. That journey that began in the back on a police car however long ago is now in the review mirror.

Anyone who has ever travelled overseas on a long holiday or spent an extended period of time away from home will know how good it is to finally come back home and sleep in your own bed. The comfort and familiarity of home is second to none. It's better than any five-star hotel, any cruise ship, any luxurious destination.

All those things are fantastic, but it will never be home or be able to provide the comfort of home. No bed will ever feel like your own bed. That feeling of relief after coming home from a holiday back to the comfort of your own home and bed is similar to how it feels coming home from prison. Only amplified by a factor of a thousand; it's that good.

Everything about coming to prison sucks. It starts with being arrested, police raiding your home, prison itself, being separated from loved ones, the stress it all causes everyone, the financial stress and loss, going through the court process, relationship pressure and breakdown... everything that's already been discussed. To finally put it all behind you and come home is such a relief.

Sitting down for a home-cooked meal with family is unbelievably satisfying and enjoyable. Good food and conversation with familiar faces is a dream. To be able to have a discussion in comfort rather than a prison visits room with guards hovering over you; to pat the dog; to meet and play with my nephews for the first time; to finally sleep with a comfortable pillow on a real mattress; to listen to my music, go for a drive, and have a shower in peace and privacy – all these little things that we all take for granted are such a welcome luxury.

Above it all, the single best part of being home is just being with family. After being separated for so long, nothing makes you appreciate your loved ones more. Losing everything and starting from scratch without a dollar to my name doesn't mean a thing to me. I don't care about that one bit. The only thing I care about losing is time with them. All I care about now is making up for that time and spending my time with the people who have suffered with me every step of the way. The financial situation and getting ahead, although important, is secondary and will fall into place with time and effort.

The family is the ones who support and visit us in prison when everyone else has forgotten about us. They stick it out through every step of the process. Family remembers birthdays when no one does. Family misses you at Christmas and worries about you when you are long forgotten by all your so-called mates. It's family who is waiting at the gate and to welcome you home and who support your progress once you're out. Without the support and love of my long-suffering family who have been through it all with me every step of the way, I don't know how I would have ever been able to make it through. Without them realising, it was them who helped me up off the cold, hard floor of rock bottom. They were my motivation to be a better father and better man. When I dreamt of coming home each and every day and night, it was my son I was thinking about, not a house. It was hugging my mum and eating her home-cooked food made with love. It was simply spending time together as a family. Happy together for good. That's home to me. That's where I want to be.

For all the love and support, I am forever grateful. It got me through and back to where I needed to be in more ways than one. I can never thank you all enough or ever repay the debt, but I will try every single day.

I love you all.

> 'Families are the compass that guide us. They are the inspiration to reach great heights, and our comfort when we occasionally falter.'
>
> —Brad Henry

Going Home

I've counted down the days
Over the long months and the years.
The day has finally come to leave.
I am excited to the point of tears.

I see my son
Outside the gates, waiting patiently to greet me.
My emotions surge, my heart races,
As the guard turns the key to free me.

What an unbelievable feeling,
Walking out the gate; I leave it all behind me.
To have prison at my back,
The world in front, welcoming me so kindly.

A huge weight lifts.
I pull into my street, as home comes into sight.
Finally, I have made it.
So many times I wished for this moment at night.

Friends and family await,
Everyone gathered to welcome me home.
To have their support
Means so much, letting me know I'm not alone.

We share a meal together.
I'm so happy we are all reunited.
I look around the table,
To have these people in my life, I'm blessed and delighted.

www.ingramcontent.com/pod-product-compliance
Lightning Source LLC
Chambersburg PA
CBHW070353120526
44590CB00014B/1120